The Art of Handmade Flowers

The Art of Handmade Flowers

MIYUKI AND TOMOKO IIDA

Photographs
by
AKIRA TSUKUI

62707

KODANSHA INTERNATIONAL LTD., Tokyo, New York & San Francisco

DISTRIBUTORS:

UNITED STATES: Kodansha International/USA Ltd., through Harper & Row, Publishers, Inc., 10 East 53rd Street, New York, New York 10022. SOUTH AMERICA: Harper & Row, Publishers, Inc., International Department. CANADA: Fitzhenry & Whiteside Limited, 150 Lesmill Road, Don Mills, Ontario M3B 2T5. MEXICO AND CENTRAL AMERICA: HARLA S.A. de C.V., Apartado 30–546, Mexico 4, D.F. UNITED KINGDOM: Phaidon Press Limited, Unit B, Ridgeway Trading Estate, Iver, Bucks SLO 9HW. EUROPE: Boxerbooks Inc., Limmatstrasse 111, 8031 Zurich. AUSTRALIA AND NEW ZEALAND: Book Wise (Australia) Pty. Ltd., 104–8 Sussex Street, Sydney 2000. ASIA: Toppan Company (S) Pte. Ltd., No. 38, Liu Fang Road, Jurong Town, Singapore 2262.

Published by Kodansha International Ltd., 12–21, Otowa 2-chome, Bunkyo-ku, Tokyo 112 and Kodansha International/USA Ltd., 10 East 53rd Street, New York, New York 10022 and 44 Montgomery Street, San Francisco, California 94104. Copyright © 1971 by Kodansha International Ltd. All rights reserved. Printed in Japan.

LCC 77–128687
ISBN 0–87011–419–0
JBC 5076-787875–2361

First edition, 1971
First paperback edition, 1980
Second printing, 1980

TABLE OF CONTENTS

PREFACE

"A heaven in a wild flower." No part of nature is more lovely than flowers, but since they fade and die, it is only natural that we should want to fix them in some enduring form.

In my own way I have tried to do this with fabrics, and have set down here the experience I have accumulated from this pastime. For after my mother died when I was young, I found considerable joy and comfort in flowers, and through this book would like to share this pleasure with others.

To make these flowers requires no special skills, only a sense of color, an eye for nature, and an interest in making things from next to nothing. Through a simple process, and using simple tools, natural flowers that are hard to cultivate, that you have seen only growing wild, or that wilt as soon as picked, will brighten your home for as long as you wish.

One recommendation, though, before you begin: keep before you, either in your mind's eye or in reality, an example of the natural bloom. Only then can you be sure to capture its true shape and coloring.

Miyuki Iida

Simple Flowers

MAKING A ROSE AND BUD

1. The parts to be used

Rose: Five large, three medium, and five small petals; one calyx; one large and four medium-sized leaves. These should be cut out from velveteen following the first of the book's patterns, together with 7 in. of light green paper-tape for the stem. For the stem, 6 in. of dark green plastic tube and 6 in. of folded wire (#24) are also required.

Bud: Two small petals and one calyx cut out from velveteen according to the same pattern. Also 8 in. of paper-tape, 7 in. of plastic tube, and 7 in. of folded wire (#24) for the stem.

The leaves and petals may be dyed, as shown here, or shaded with crayon or poster color.

4–6. Hollowing the base of a large petal. This process may be carried out in three different ways: first, by pressing the petal, placed on foam rubber, with a heated teaspoon; by stretching and pressing it with the fingers; or, yet again, by slitting the base of the petal, crossing the two flaps over each other, and gluing them together.

On smaller petals, the hollow should be made not at the base but nearer the center of the fabric.

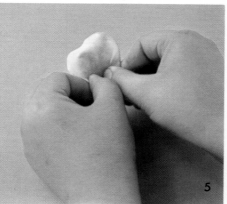
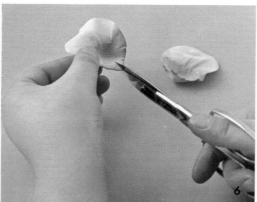

2. For the stems, pass the folded wire through the tube and loop the end of the wire over the top rim. Now wrap the tube spirally with the paper-tape glued along one side.

3. The hearts of the flower and bud are formed by gluing absorbent cotton in an oval-shaped ball round the tip of the stem.

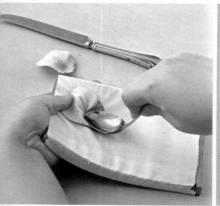
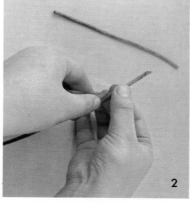
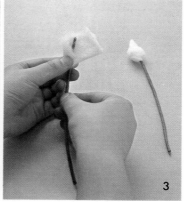

7–8. The top edges of large and medium-sized petals are curled with either moistened fingertips or the side of a heated fork.

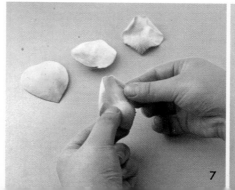
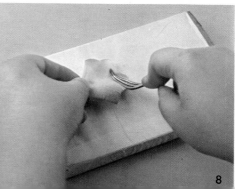

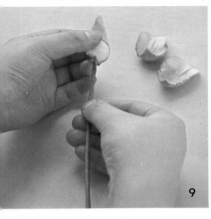
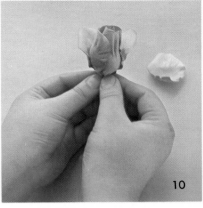

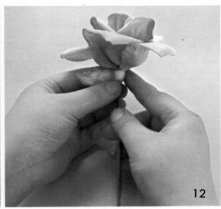

9

10

11

12

9. To form the flower's inner spiral of petals, glue the whole of **one small petal** round the absorbent cotton and arrange the other four around it in an alternating pattern, lightly gluing only their lower half.

10. The medium-sized petals are then added by gluing their bases to the small petals.

11. Round the flower, space the five large, open petals so that their edges overlap, and glue their bases to the bottom of the flower.

12. Wrap and glue a strip of absorbent cotton round the top of the stem as a basis for the calyx.

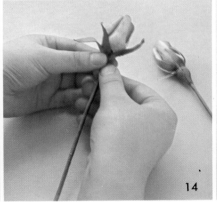

13

14

15

15. On the back of each leaf, paste wire wrapped with green paper-tape, allowing the wire to extend about 2 in. beyond the base of the leaf. Then join three leaves together, the large leaf placed centrally, by wrapping with light green paper-tape, glued on one side.

17. The completed rose and bud.

13. The calyx is then pasted onto the absorbent cotton.

14. The bud's calyx is formed in the same way. Notice that of the two petals, **one tightly encloses the heart of absorbent cotton, the other remains relatively open, with curled edges.**

The other rosebud shown demonstrates a method of pinching the neck of the calyx with wire to swell its base.

16. With a knife, make veins on both sides of each leaf. This process should be done on foam rubber.

16

17

Made in the same way as the preceding rose, White Night roses combine with other varieties in an abundant arrangement.

Marguerites, native to the Canary Islands, here have petals of white cotton, set off by dark green leafage at the center of the bunch.

◁ Feathery carnations of pale pink silk show amidst a tangle of baby's breath. The carnations' inner petals should be a shade darker than the rest of the flower.

Ribboned carnations can be used either as dress accessories or to add a special touch to wrapped gifts.

These cornflowers, sometimes called bachelor's buttons, are made of blue silk. A bunch of them is enhanced by varying the depth of the petals' blue or introducing pink and white varieties.

Field poppies, their red silk petals a splash ▷ of vivid color, are perhaps the simplest of flowers to make. In contrast, orchids display their elaborate forms above them.

◁ The Cape jasmine is one of the most beautiful of all gardenias. A spray of them, without leaves, can be used with effect to decorate wall hangings and mirrors.

Spiralling tendrils of wire wrapped with paper-tape contribute to the realism of these sweet peas of white, pink, and mauve silk.

19

With long, fluted coronas of deep yellow velveteen and petals of white or yellow cotton, daffodils are best suited to a tall, plain vase.

From a hanging wall vase, nasturtiums trail their flowers of brilliant, striped velveteen. The natural flower is a climber native to Peru.

With showy mauve, magenta, purple, or red bracts enclosing small flowers, bougainvilleas might be placed around arches or on pergolas to provide a touch of tropical color.

Clematis has no petals but ▷ large white or colored sepals. The flowers are best arranged on small trellises or in wicker baskets.

The heads of hydrangeas turn from white or pale pink to a delicate, purplish blue. These are composed of two or more mixed fabrics.

Sunflowers have long, rough stems and large heads, sometimes a foot or more wide. When mature they have dark brown hearts, here made of dyed absorbent cotton. The smaller flowers would be an attractive decoration for a straw hat.

The dark red, convoluted heads and drooping leaves of cockscombs are not easy to make but are unusually natural in appearance.

Poinsettias with leaves and bracts of gold and silver lamé make an uncommon Christmas decoration.

◁ A bouquet of wild orchids with cotton, rayon velvet, and satin petals, together with roses of white gauze and pink or green rayon, make handsome dress accessories.

A White Swan rose and two camellias with buds, their petals of velveteen combined with other fabrics, are yet another choice of decoration.

Variations on traditional dress ornaments are the carnations, sweet peas, and rose of black georgette pictured here.

29

An indoor garden of arum lilies and begonias: the arums, made of white velveteen, are characterized by a central yellow spadix of dyed absorbent cotton.

The canna, a native of warm climates, has spikelike buds and a cluster of bright yellow, red, or orange flowers. The red and yellow ones reproduced here are made of rayon velvet.

Sometimes called a winter cherry, the Chinese lantern plant has scarlet or deep orange bracts enclosing a round fruit. Below them are pinecones, whose velveteen scales are flecked with gold paint.

None of these imaginative blooms is dyed or colored by hand. The pink rose and blue and white marguerites are of striped cotton; the other flowers are cut out from dress material of matching design.

33

Thin PVC of varying shades provides the basic material for these oriental poppies and marguerites, as well as the rose and exotic golden flower.

Crepe paper flowers, such as ▷ these oriental poppies and roses, lend themselves to exuberant colors. A double-sided paper can be used to novel effect.

34

Flowers, or merely shaped petals, pasted onto head-bands are not difficult to make and may be designed to match a particular dress color. Only the pink rose and pale green headbands are provided with patterns.

Model Displays

A cardinal is perched on a lower limb of this autumnal composition that includes asters, lotus pods, spindle-tree twigs, and yellow and red feather cockscombs.

◁ In this sumptuous arrangement at least eight varieties of orchids are represented. They are an exceptionally hard flower to reproduce, both in form and coloring.

Reminiscent of old Dutch flower paintings, this display features lilacs, old-fashioned roses, bouvardia, and buttercups.

41

Sprays of Japanese flowering cherry: interspersed among the double-headed, white blossoms are pink and pale yellow petals.

Flowers and grasses of the field —gentians, marigolds, barley, and daisies, among others—are represented in these framed compositions.

Flowers for a wedding: lilies of the valley, carnations, orchises, marguerites, and roses are formed into bouquets and dress ornaments.

44

First Steps
and
Instructions

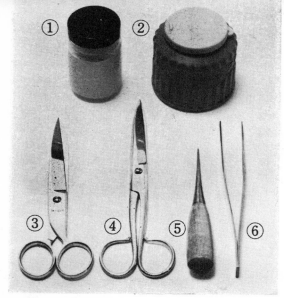

1. Chemical glue   2. Paste   3. Scissors for cutting
wire   4. Scissors for cutting fabric   5. Awl
6. Tweezers

TOOLS

Scissors: Two pairs are needed, one for cutting fabrics, the
other for cutting wire; small pincers would serve the latter
purpose equally well. The tips of the scissors can be used to
crease petals or make veins on leaves.

Awls: One of the small, straight kind is needed, principally
for piercing the center of calyxes and sets of petals, but also
for curling the edges of petals by rolling them over its thin
metal shaft. This too can be done with a sewing awl, the curved
shaft of which is pressed along the petals' edges (the shaft being
heated before use).

Small fork: The tips, pinched together, provide another means
of making veins or creases. When heated, the tips are used
to hollow small petals.

Table knife: The round, heated end of the handle can be used
to press petals and leaves into curves. Veins and creases can
also be made with the blunt edge of the blade.

Teaspoon: When heated, the back serves to curve the parts
of larger flowers.

Foam rubber: When creasing or curving the parts of a flower,
always place them on a piece of foam rubber, about 1/2 in.
thick and measuring 4 in. × 6 in. This prevents the fabric from
being torn and allows one to control the pressure one is applying. The foam rubber should be covered with a thin cotton
cloth.

MATERIALS

Thick, white, cotton thread: This is used for the stamens of some
flowers (baby's breath and hydrangeas, for example). It should
first be stiffened with starch, then cut into suitable lengths
according to the flower, with a small drop of white glue
placed on the tip of each piece in the shape of a match head.
A very narrow strip of thin white paper, twisted tightly into
a strand and starched, could be used instead of cotton thread.

Fabrics: Those recommended in the book's patterns are velveteen, rayon velvet, cotton, silk, rayon, georgette, and PVC
(the initials stand for polyvinyl chloride, the resinous coating

1. Varieties of plastic tube   2. Thin, white and green
wire (the wire shown here is wrapped with paper to
prevent glue from weakening it)   3. Varieties of
paper-tape

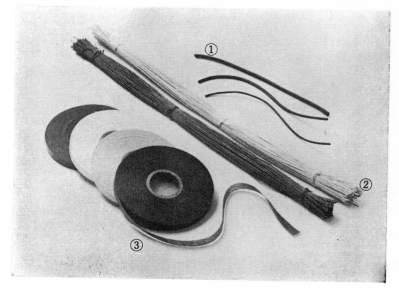

given to certain textiles. If this fabric is not obtainable, substitute thin imitation leather). There is no reason, however, why you should not experiment with other fabrics, whether plain, striped, or laminated, so as to find the ideal texture or to vary the appearance of the flowers.

Wire: Wrapped with paper-tape or a strip of fabric (called "stem fabric" in the patterns), this serves as a stem for most flowers and also as a support for leaves and petals. The guage of the wire (#20, #22, #24) differs, naturally, according to the flower.

Plastic tube: With wire passed through it to make it firm, the tube provides a more rigid type of stem.

Paper-tape: Used to wrap wire. Like the strip of stem fabric, it should first have glue applied to one side of it, then be wound round in an even spiral, with the edges of each coil slightly overlapping. The recommended width of the tape is about 1/3 in.

Absorbent cotton (cotton wool): This is added in order to swell the base of some calyxes and flowers and also to form the inner core of buds.

Glue or paste: Any clear, quick-drying variety is suitable.

PREPARATION

Starching: All fabrics, with the exception of stiff ones like PVC, must be starched before being cut out. This prevents the edges from fraying and also prolongs the original shape of flowers and leaves.

To make the starch (of ordinary thickness), mix one tablespoon of cornstarch with a tablespoon of water. Boil 4/5 of a cup of water in a pot, add the cornstarch solution, and continue heating over a low flame until thick, stirring constantly. Remove from the heat, add one tablespoon of glue, mix well, and allow to cool.

Before cutting out the fabric, fasten it with pins onto a board with the back of the fabric facing outward. Then apply the starch with a brush, wipe the fabric lightly with a moistened cloth, and leave to dry. Keep the board flat throughout.

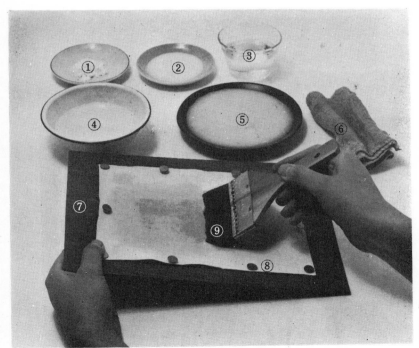

1. 1 tablespoon of cornstarch 2. 1 tablespoon of glue
3. 4/5 of a cup of water 4. Mixture of cornstarch and water 5. Starch after boiling 6. Damp cloth
7. Board 8. Fabric fastened on the board with pins
9. Brush

Cutting: First make a tracing of each part of the pattern, taking care to include in your tracings the arrows shown in the pattern. Then pin the tracings onto the back of the starched fabric, with the arrows parallel to the lengthwise grain, and cut out each piece. When very thin fabric is used and the petals are of the same size (as in field poppies), cut out all the petals at one time, placing the fabric in layers.

As a rule, calyxes, petals, and leaves have a diagonal grain, as this allows flexibility in their shaping, but in the case of narrow petals joined to one strip of fabric (as in marguerites), as well as strips of stamens and stem fabric, the grain is usually vertical.

Coloring: All handmade flowers, even white ones, are enhanced by careful shading in an appropriate color.

In the instructions provided in this book, the recommended means of coloring are crayons, pastels, felt pens, or poster colors. To obtain a more natural effect, however, the reader should consider dyeing the fabrics—a worthwhile, if more time-consuming, process. To do this, a number of small white plates are needed, together with blotting paper, brushes, direct dyes, absorbent cotton, and a mixture of liquid detergent and water (one or two drops of detergent for every 1 1/2 cups of water). Place a little dye (in powdered form) in a small plate, add a little hot water, and mix well. Should the color need deepening, mix in two or three more dyes of a slightly darker shade. To produce a dark, bluish red, for example, mix together red, purple, and rhodamine dyes.

When thin materials are used, place three or four petals one on top of the other and dip them in the mixture of detergent and water with a pair of tweezers. Remove and separate the petals, placing them on blotting paper to absorb the liquid. Join them into a set again and dip the petals in the dye solution. Remove them and allow each to dry separately on the blotting paper.

When thicker fabrics are used, lightly moisten each petal with absorbent cotton dipped in the mixture of detergent and water. Then brush the dye onto the petals and allow them to dry completely.

To dye only the edges of petals, first moisten the edges in the mixture of detergent and water, then dip them in the dye solution.

FURTHER PROCESSES

Curving: After starching and cutting out the parts (and dyeing them if so desired), place a damp cloth over them and pat lightly over the cloth to moisten. Remove the cloth and place the cutouts on the piece of foam rubber. At the appropriate stage in the instructions, press on the specified areas with one of the tools recommended.

Leaf supports: Wire, wrapped with paper-tape, is glued down the center of the back of each leaf and extended beyond the leaf's base to serve as a stem. On broad leaves, other pieces of wire may be added as further supports (one example is shown in the illustration below). To avoid a too rigid effect, no piece of wire should come closer than 1/6 in. to a leaf's edges.

Veins: After attaching the leaf supports, place the leaves on the foam rubber and make veins (on both sides) corresponding to those shown in the pattern. Lengthwise veins should start from the base, slanting ones from the center, and both should become softer toward the edges. A selection of different types of veining is shown in the illustration below.

Note. To gain experience, the beginner is advised to start with marguerites or pink carnations, these being some of the easiest flowers to make.

VEINS

LEAF SUPPORTS
(on back only)

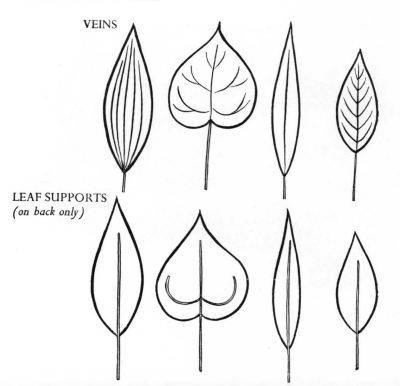

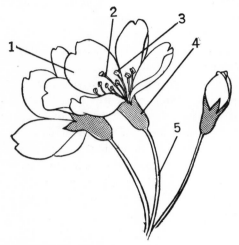

CHERRY BLOSSOM WITH BUD
1. Petals
2. Pistil
3. Stamens
4. Calyx
5. Stem

POINSETTIA
1. Flowers
2. Bract
3. Stem
4. Leaf

MARGUERITE

MATERIALS (*for one flower and two leaves*)
Petals: White cotton.
Stamens: White velveteen or thick white cotton.
Calyx: Green velveteen.
Leaves: Green velveteen or rayon velvet, wire (#24), and green
       paper-tape.
Stem: 1 ft. of wire (#22), and green velveteen.

Working from the pattern on page 90, cut out the appropriate fabrics for one strip of petals and one of stamens, one calyx, two leaves, as well as a strip of stem fabric (green velveteen).

Make slits in the stamen, calyx, and petal fabrics, and serrate the latter's edge, as shown in the same pattern.

Apply glue halfway along the back of the stem fabric. Bend the tip of the stem's wire. Then, leaving the tip bare, wrap the stem fabric (with the back inside) spirally round the upper half of the wire (illustration 1). The lower half of the wire is left uncovered until the leaves are added.

Hook the tip of the wire in a slit at one end of the strip of stamens (illustration 2). Roll up the strip evenly round the wire, applying glue along the lower half of the fabric (illustration 3).

Press the back of each petal with a heated knife-handle or the tips of a fork to curve, and make creases, as shown in illustration 4, on back and front. Make a row of running stitches 1/6 in. from the bottom of the petal fabric (illustration 4). Then gather the stitches (illustration 5), so that the lower part of the petal fabric may then be glued neatly round the rolled stamens without its ends overlapping.

Pierce the center of the calyx with an awl, pass the stem through the hole, and glue the calyx (with the back inside) round the bottom of the flower (illustration 6).

As illustration 7 makes clear, glue a piece of wire (#24), wrapped with green paper-tape, along the center of the back of each leaf, allowing it to extend about 1 1/2 in. beyond the base. Then glue a second, V-shaped piece of wire over it.

Make veins as shown in the pattern on both sides of each leaf. Then join the leaves' short stems onto the main stem by wrapping with the rest of the stem fabric (applying glue along the back). The leaves, spaced slightly apart, should be arranged on opposite sides of the stem.

Completed marguerites are shown in the color plate on page 13.

N.B. Buds are made with exactly the same pattern and process, except that the petals, after being curved, are folded inward around the stamens (illustration 8).

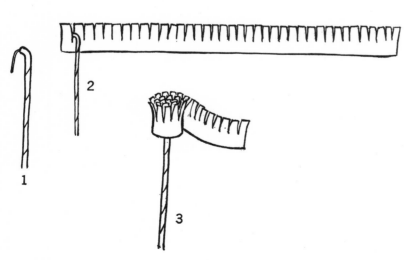

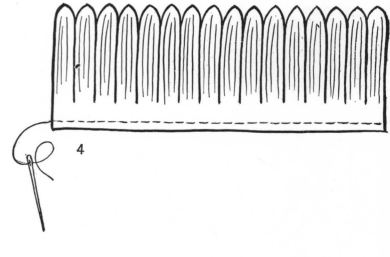

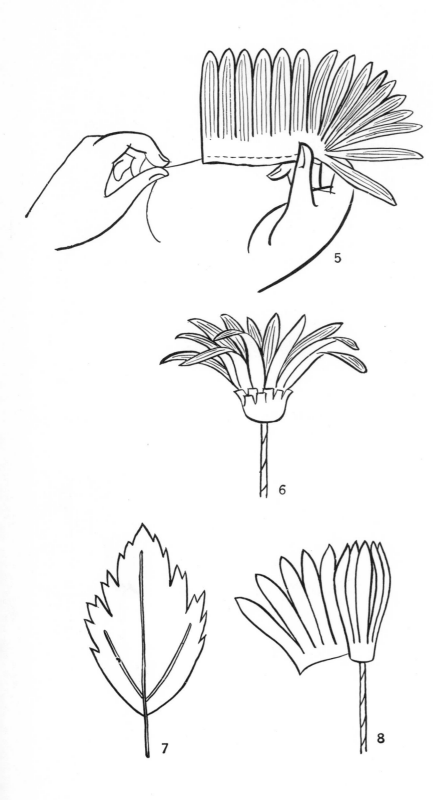

5

6

7

8

BABY'S BREATH

MATERIALS *(for ten flowers)*
Flowers: White velveteen or cotton.
Stamens: White cotton thread and white glue (see page 46).
Make ten stamens, each about 1 1/2 in. long.
Stem: 1 ft. of wire (#22), and pale green paper-tape.

Cut out ten flowers according to the pattern on page 91. Then moisten them lightly with a damp towel.

Press the center of each flower with the heated tips of a small fork to make a shallow dip. Pierce each center with an awl and pass a stamen through the hole (illustration 1). Glue the head of the stamen to the flower.

To make the spray of flowers shown in illustration 2, first cut the stem wire into two pieces, 8 in. long, and join them to form a forked stem. Apply glue to several strips of pale green paper-tape. Then take two flowers, and with the paper-tape wrap the bottom of their stamens onto the tip of each branch of the stem. Winding the paper-tape spirally down the rest of the stem add on the other flowers in the same way.

Examples of the completed flowers are shown in the color plate on page 14.

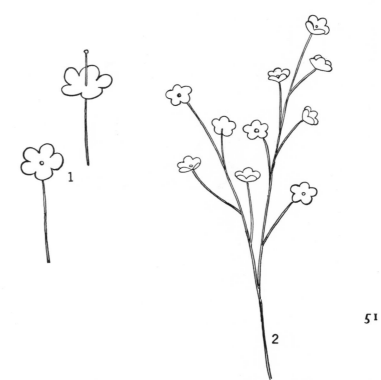

1

2

51

PINK CARNATION

MATERIALS (*for one flower*)

Petals: Thin pink silk or cotton. (Any other color, of course, may be used for carnations.)

Calyx: Same as for petals (or light green silk instead), and absorbent cotton.

Stem: 1 ft. of plastic tube, 1 ft. of wire (#22), and light green paper-tape.

Cut out one calyx according to the pattern on page 91. Then cut out three sets of petals (each set having eight petals), and make slits as shown between each of the petals. Do not serrate the petals' edges until each set has been folded into one petal, so that the same fringe can be cut for all eight petals at one time.

Open out each of the folded sets of petals once, and press the points marked in illustration 1 with the heated handle of a knife to make a wavy edge—the shaded areas should be pressed on one side of the fabric, the unshaded areas on the other side. Now open out the sets of petals completely. Then fold only one set in half again, in such a way that its petals are visible alternately (illustration 2).

Pass the stem wire through the tube, bend the wire's tip, and loop it over the rim of the tube.

Bend the tip of the tube. Apply glue to the bottom center of one side of the folded set of petals (shown as the shaded area in illustration 2). Place the tube's bent tip in the middle of this glued area and roll the folded set of petals round it into a trumpet shape (illustration 3).

Lay the remaining two sets of petals together so that their petals appear alternately. Pierce their centers and pass the stem through the hole (illustration 4). Then glue their centers together, stick these sets to the base of the one already in place, and push their petals upward.

Finally, glue a thin strip of absorbent cotton round the lower part of the outer set of petals; then stick the calyx round the absorbent cotton (illustration 5).

Completed pink carnations are shown in the color plate on page 14.

N.B. The blue and black carnations in the plates on pages 15 and 29 are made in exactly the same way.

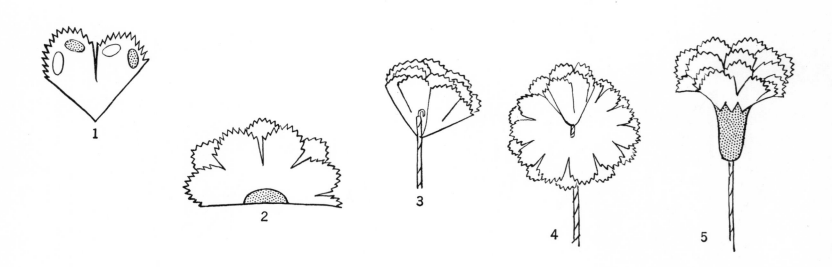

CORNFLOWER

MATERIALS (*for one flower*)
Petals: Thin silk in a suitable shade of blue, pink, or white.
Stamens: Thick cotton of same color as petals.
Calyx: Green cotton.
Stem: Green cotton. Also 7 in. of wire (#24).

Cut out the fabrics for one of each part of the flower according to the pattern on page 92. Cut slits as shown, making sure the strip of petal fabric is folded in half before serrating its edge and cutting the slits.

Bend the tip of the wire for the stem and hook it in a slit at one end of the stamen fabric. Apply glue along the lower half of the stamen fabric and roll the fabric up evenly round the top of the wire.

Now slide one side of the folded petal fabric down 1/8 in. and make a row of running stitches 1/8 in. from the bottom (illustration 1). Then gather the stitches so that the lower half of the petal fabric may then be glued round the roll of stamens without its ends overlapping.

Pierce the center of the calyx with an awl, pass the stem through the hole, and glue the calyx round the base of the flower (illustration 2).

Stick one end of the stem fabric obliquely to the bottom of the calyx and glue the rest spirally down the stem wire (illustration 3). Open out the petals.

To combine a number of cornflowers (illustration 4), join the stems of three or four flowers to 10 in. of wire (#22) by wrapping the stems and wire with green paper-tape or ribbon.

The color plate on page 16 shows how the completed flowers should look.

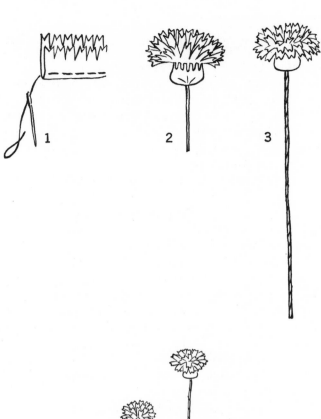

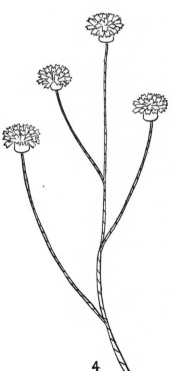

FIELD POPPY

MATERIALS (*for one flower and two leaves*)

Petals: Thin red silk or rayon, wire (#24), and red paper-tape.

Disk: Thin, light green silk or rayon, and absorbent cotton.
    (The disk is the round, flattened head of the stem.)

Stamens: Black velveteen.

Leaves: Green rayon velvet (or velveteen), wire (#24), and
    green paper-tape.

Stem: Light green rayon velvet and 1 ft. of wire (#22).

Cut out according to the pattern on page 93 four petals, one large and one small leaf, two sets of stamens (making slits as shown), and the stem and disk fabrics.

Color the base of one side of each petal black, as shown by the shaded area in the pattern. This will be their inner side.

Bend the tip of the stem wire and glue round it a small ball of absorbent cotton (1/5 in. diameter). Then apply glue to one side of the disk fabric and fold it over the absorbent cotton.

Pierce the centers of the two sets of stamens with an awl; pass the stem wire through the holes (the front of the stamen fabric face up); stick the two sets together, and then onto the disk (illustrations 1 and 2).

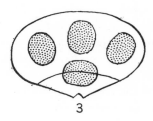

To curve each petal, press their inner sides with the heated handle of a knife on the four places marked in illustration 3.

Then glue wire (#24), wrapped with red paper-tape, from the base to the center of the outer side of each petal.

As shown in illustration 4, take two petals and glue them opposite each other onto the base of the stamens. In the same way, attach the remaining petals to cover the gaps between the first two.

Glue wire (#24), wrapped with green paper-tape, along the center of the back of each leaf, extending it about 1 in. beyond the base of the leaf.

Make veins, as shown in the pattern, on both sides of each leaf.

Then, when gluing the stem fabric (with the back inside) spirally down the main stem, add on the leaves' short stems.

The color plate on page 17 shows a number of completed field poppies.

CAPE JASMINE

MATERIALS (*for one flower, one bud, and three leaves*)
Flower petals: White velveteen, wire (#24), and white paper-tape.
Bud petal: White velveteen. Also absorbent cotton.
Stamens: White velveteen.
Calyxes: Light green rayon velvet.
Leaves: Green rayon velvet, wire (#24), and green paper-tape.
Flower stem: Grayish brown velveteen and 1 ft. 8 in. of wire (#24).
Bud stem: Grayish brown velveteen and 8 in. of wire (#24).

Working from the pattern on page 94, cut out for the flower one set of petals and one set of stamens (making slits in both as shown), one small leaf and two larger ones, one calyx, and a strip of stem fabric. For the bud, cut out one calyx, one triangular petal, and stem fabric of the same width as the flower's but only 5 in. long.

Fold the wire for the flower's stem in half. Wind the longer strip of stem fabric, after applying glue along the back of it, spirally round 1 in. of one end of this folded wire. The rest of the wire is left bare until the leaves and bud are added.

Bend the tip of the wrapped part of the stem and hook it in a slit at one end of the stamen fabric. Then roll up the stamen fabric after applying glue along its lower half. Color the tips of the stamens yellow.

With pale green poster color or crayon, lightly color both sides of the flower's petals from the base toward the center, and the bud's petal (on only the front of the fabric) from the top toward the center.

Now glue wire (#24), wrapped with white paper-tape, along the center of the back of each of the flower's petals to within 1/8 in. of the top (see illustration 1). Make sure the wire does not overlap the base of the petals.

With moistened fingers, bend the flower's petals outward. Make a row of running stitches 1/8 in. from their base (illustration 2). Gather the stitches so that the strip of petals may then be glued (with the back outside) round the roll of stamens without its ends overlapping. Then stick the calyx (back inside) round the bottom of the petals and just covering the top of the stem.

Fold the bud's stem wire in half. Glue the shorter strip of stem fabric (back inside) spirally down the wire. Round the tip of this stem, stick an oval-shaped ball of absorbent cotton. Then place it centrally on the back of the bud's petal (illustration 3) and fold the petal's two halves over each other (illustration 4). Apply glue along the petal's lower inside edge and pinch it in round the stem (illustration 5).

Add the bud's calyx in the same way as for the flower.

Down the center of the back of each leaf, glue wire (#24) wrapped with green paper-tape, and make veins (as shown in the pattern) on both sides of the leaves with the blunt edge of a knife.

Join the stems of the bud and leaves to the flower's stalk by wrapping with the rest of the stem fabric in an even spiral.

Completed Cape jasmines are shown in the color plate on page 18.

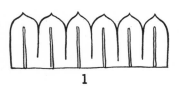

1

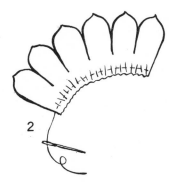

2

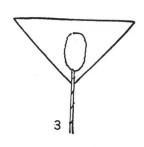

3

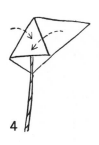

4

5

SWEET PEA

MATERIALS (*for one flower*)
Petals: Thin cotton, silk, rayon, or nylon of appropriate color.
Heart: Rayon velvet of darker shade than petals, and absorbent cotton.
Calyx: Light green cotton.
Stem: Light green cotton, and 1 ft. of wire (#22).

Following the pattern on page 95, cut out one calyx, one large and one small petal, one heart, and a strip of stem fabric.

Apply glue to the back of the stem fabric and wind it spirally down the stem wire.

Bend the tip of the wire and glue absorbent cotton round it to form the basis of the heart. Then glue the back of the piece of rayon velvet for the heart onto the absorbent cotton (illustration 1), fold the piece in half (illustration 2), and stick its edges together.

Lay the two petals together. With a knife, make three fine lines on the base of the smaller petal and press its upper part with a heated spoon or knife-handle to curve (see the shaded areas in illustration 3). Turn the larger petal round and glue the bases of the petals together.

Fold the lower half of the joined petals (the larger petal on the outside) round the heart (illustration 4), and glue the bottom of the heart and petals together.

Stick the calyx round the base of the flower, as shown in illustration 5.

Examples of the finished flowers are shown in the color plate on page 19.

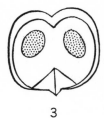

3

4

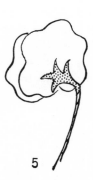

5

1

2

DAFFODIL

MATERIALS (*for one flower and one leaf*)

Petals: Yellow cotton, wire (#24), and yellow paper-tape.

Stamens: White rayon velvet.

Corona: Deep yellow rayon velvet. (The corona is the cylindrical part in the center of the petals.)

Bract: Thin, light brown silk.

Calyx: Thin, light green silk.

Leaf: Green velveteen or thick green cotton, and wire (#24).

Stem: 10 in. of plastic tube (1/8 in. diameter), 10 in. of wire (#22), and green paper-tape.

Cut out two sets of petals, one set of stamens (making slits as shown), one calyx, a bract, a corona, and a leaf, according to the pattern on page 96.

Pass the stem wire through the plastic tube and bend the wire's tip over the rim of the tube. Apply glue along one side of the stamen fabric, place the tip of the tube at one end of it, and roll the fabric up tightly round the top of the wire. Then stick one end of a length of green paper-tape obliquely to the base of the rolled stamens, and glue the rest spirally down the plastic tube (illustration 1).

As shown in illustration 2, make creases with the tip of a knife on the back of the corona fabric and make a row of running stitches 1/6 in. from the base. About 1/3 in. above the stitches, stretch the fabric with moistened fingers to create a slight bulge. Then glue the edges of the corona together in a cylindrical shape (the back of the fabric inside).

Pass the stem through the corona and draw the thread of the running stitches to gather tightly (illustration 3). Glue the base of the stamens inside the corona; the tips of the stamens should be about 1/5 in. below the corona's rim.

On the center of the back of each petal, glue wire (#24) wrapped with yellow paper-tape (illustration 4). Then make central creases on both sides of each petal and cut small slits at the base, as shown in the pattern.

Glue each set of petals round the base of the corona, arranging them so that their petals alternate (illustration 5).

Following illustration 6, stick the calyx round the bottom of the flower and about 1 in. down the stem; then glue the bract onto the stem at a point about 3/4 in. below the calyx, and bend the stem at the calyx.

Now stick wire (#24), wrapped with green paper-tape, down the center of the back of the leaf and make a central vein on the front. Apply glue to green paper-tape and wrap the leaf onto the stem with it.

A bunch of completed daffodils is shown on page 20.

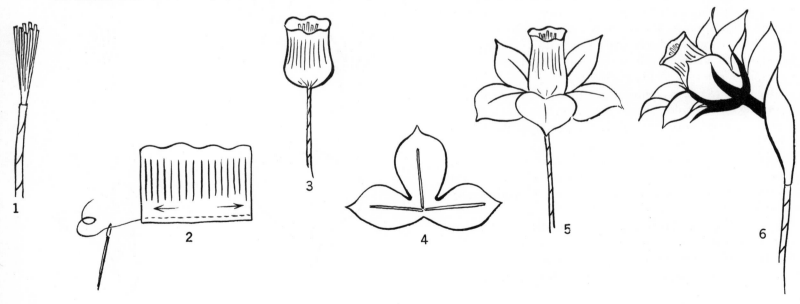

NASTURTIUM

MATERIALS (*for one flower, one bud, and three leaves*)

Flower petals: Red or yellow velveteen, wire (#24), and red or yellow paper-tape.

Bud petal: Red or yellow velveteen. Also wire (#24) and green paper-tape.

Calyxes: Thin cream-colored cotton.

Leaves: Green velveteen, wire (#24), and green paper-tape.

Main stem: 8 in. of wire (#24), and green paper-tape.

According to the pattern on page 97, cut out three large and two small petals for the flower; one petal for the bud; one large and one small calyx; one large, one medium, and one small leaf; and a strip of stamens (making slits as shown).

Glue green paper-tape spirally round a 4 in. piece of wire (#24). Bend the wire's tip and hook it in a slit at one end of the stamen fabric. Then apply glue along the lower half of one side of the stamen fabric and roll it up tightly round the top of the wire. Color the tips of the stamens yellow.

With a felt pen, make stripes (red on yellow petals, black on red ones), as shown in illustration 1, on the front of each of the flower's petals.

To create gentle folds on the top edges of these petals, twist the fabric with moistened fingers at the points shown as dotted areas in illustration 2. Then hollow the center of the front of each petal by pressing and stretching with your fingers the part shown as a shaded area. The result should resemble the petal shown sideview in illustration 3.

Glue wire (#24), wrapped with paper-tape (red or yellow depending on the color chosen for the petals), onto the back of each large and small petal from the center to the base and 2 in. beyond the base (illustration 4).

Apply glue to the lower part of the front of the two small petals and attach them side by side to the roll of stamens. Then add the three large ones in the same way to complete the flower's head.

For the bud, glue green paper-tape spirally round 4 in. of wire (#24) to serve as a stem. Then stick the wrapped wire from the base to the center of the back of the bud's petal. Fold the petal loosely into a trumpet shape and lightly stick down the free edge.

On the back of each calyx, press the shaded area shown in illustration 5 with the heated handle of a knife. Then, holding the fringed end of the calyx in one hand, with the other pull the rest of the calyx downward to curve (illustration 6).

Glue absorbent cotton round the bottom of the flower and bud, and stick the calyxes over it (the smaller calyx for the bud, the larger one for the flower). Bend the tops of the stems as shown in illustration 7.

With a knife or the tips of a fork, make veins (as shown in the pattern) on both sides of each leaf. Then, using illustration 8 as a guide, glue one piece of wire (#24), wrapped with green paper-tape, across the back of each leaf; now stick a second, wrapped piece of wire (4 in. long) from the top to the center of the leaf, leaving the rest of this piece unfastened to serve as a stem.

Finally join the stems of the flower, bud, and leaves onto the main stem by wrapping spirally with green paper-tape (applying glue to one side of the tape). One way of arranging them is shown in illustration 9.

For examples of completed nasturtiums, see the color plate on page 21.

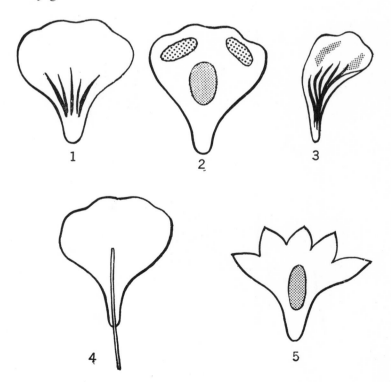

58

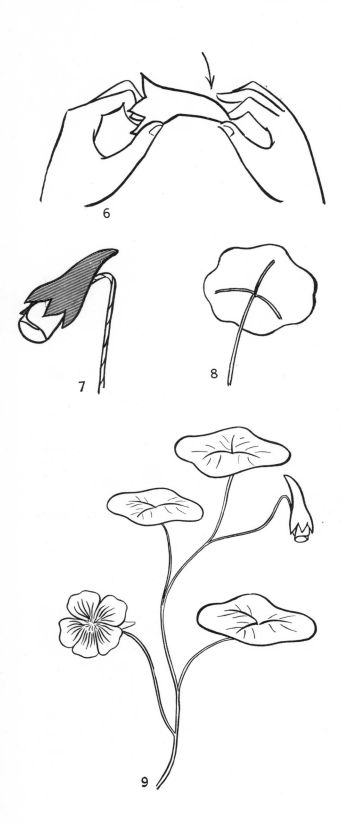

6

7

8

9

BOUGAINVILLEA

MATERIALS (*for two blooms and three leaves*)
Bracts: Red rayon.
Open flowers: Yellow rayon velvet, wire (#24), and light brown
paper-tape.
Closed flowers: Light brown velveteen or cotton, wire (#24),
and light brown paper-tape.
Leaves: Green velveteen or cotton, wire (#24), and green
paper-tape.
Main stem: 10 in. of wire (#22), and light brown paper-tape.

First see the plate on page 22 for reference to the form of
bougainvilleas. Then, using the pattern on page 98, cut out
three large and three small bracts; two open flowers; two large
and two small closed flowers; one large and two small leaves.
At the same time, as the pattern shows, cut slits along one
edge of the open flowers and three slits at the top of the closed
ones.

Glue light brown paper-tape round each of two 3 in. pieces
of wire (#24). Bend the tips of the wires and hook them in
the slits at one end of each open flower. Then apply glue along
the lower half of the back of each open flower and roll it up
tightly round the top of the wire.

To make a deep hollow down the back of each closed flower,
press the parts shown as shaded areas in illustration 1 with the
heated handle of a knife. Then glue a curved piece of wire
(#24), wrapped with light brown paper-tape, down the middle
of each hollow (illustration 2).

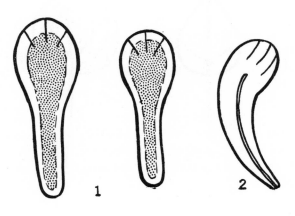

1

2

On the center of the back of the bracts, glue wire (#24), wrapped with red paper-tape, extending it 2 in. beyond the base of the bracts. Next glue a V-shaped piece of wire (#24) over this central wire in the same way as for a leaf (see illustration 3).

With the blunt edge of a knife, make veins (as shown in the pattern) on both sides of the bracts.

Glue the small closed flowers, facing in toward each other, onto the wire below one open flower—the tops of the closed flowers should be about 1/5 in. below the top of the open one. Then do the same with the larger closed flowers and the remaining open flower.

Round the small closed flowers, glue three of the smaller-sized bracts (the wire supports on the outside), and curl them inward slightly (illustration 4). Then apply glue to green paper-tape and wrap the bracts' stems together with it. Repeat these processes with the larger bracts and closed flowers.

Down the center of the back of each leaf, stick wire (#24) wrapped with green paper-tape, extending the wire 2 in. beyond the base of the leaf. Over this wire, glue another wrapped piece, bent into a V-shape (see illustration 3). Then make veins (as shown in the pattern) on both sides of the leaves.

To join the smaller bloom's stem to the top of the 10 in. main stem, glue light brown paper-tape spirally round both stems. Winding the tape down the rest of the main stem, add on the two small leaves, the other bloom, and the large leaf in that order (illustration 5).

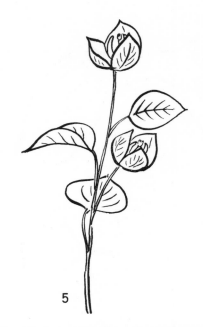

5

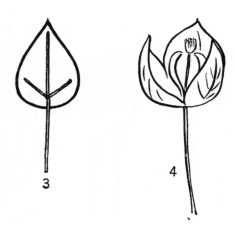

3   4

CLEMATIS

MATERIALS (*for one flower, one bud, and eight leaves*)
Flower sepals: Violet-colored velveteen, paper-tape of same shade, and wire (#24).
Inner stamens: Light green velveteen or thick cotton.
Outer stamens: Thick white cotton.
Bud sepals: Thick white cotton, wire (#24), and absorbent cotton.
Leaves: Green rayon velvet or velveteen. Also wire (#24) and green paper-tape.
Main stem: Light brown cotton and 8 in. of wire (#22).

Cut out one of each set of sepals (one for the bud, the other for the flower), one of each sort of stamens (cutting slits as shown), one strip of main stem fabric, and eight leaves—two of each size marked A, B, C, D—according to the pattern on page 99.

Color the tips of the inner stamens pale violet.

After cutting off 4 in. of wire (#24) for the flower's upper stem, glue light green paper-tape spirally round it, leaving the tip of the wire bare. Then bend the bare tip and hook it in a slit at one end of the inner stamens. Apply glue along their lower half and roll them up round the wire.

Make a hole in the center of the outer stamens, pass the upper stem through it, and glue the outer stamens to the bottom of the rolled inner stamens. Slightly open out the bunched inner stamens.

With poster color or chalk, make a white six-pointed star on the front center of the flower's set of sepals (illustration 1). Then glue wire (#24), wrapped with violet paper-tape, onto the back of each sepal (as shown in illustration 2), and press the points marked in the same illustration with the heated handle of a knife to curve. On the front of each sepal, make three creases with a knife (see illustration 3).

After piercing the center of the flower's set of sepals with an awl, pass the upper stem through the hole and glue the center of the sepals to the bottom of the stamens (illustration 4).

With pale violet poster color or crayon, lightly shade the upper half of the front of the bud's set of three sepals. Then press the back of each sepal to round (illustration 5).

After gluing light green paper-tape round 4 in. of wire (#24) for the bud's stem, stick a small oval-shaped ball of absorbent cotton onto the tip of the wire. Then fold the sepals (with the back inside) round the absorbent cotton, as shown in illustrations 6 and 7, and glue the sepals' edges together.

On the center of the back of each leaf, glue wire (#24) wrapped with light green paper-tape, extending it about 2 in. beyond the leaf's base. Make veins corresponding to those shown in the pattern on both sides of each leaf with a knife.

Apply glue to a length of light brown paper-tape. With this, wrap the flower's upper stem onto the 8 in. wire (#22) for the main stem. Wind the tape spirally down the rest of the wire, adding on the stems of the bud and leaves. Arrange the leaves in pairs, one leaf opposite the other, with the smaller pairs toward the top or the main stem.

The finished flowers are shown in the plate on page 23.

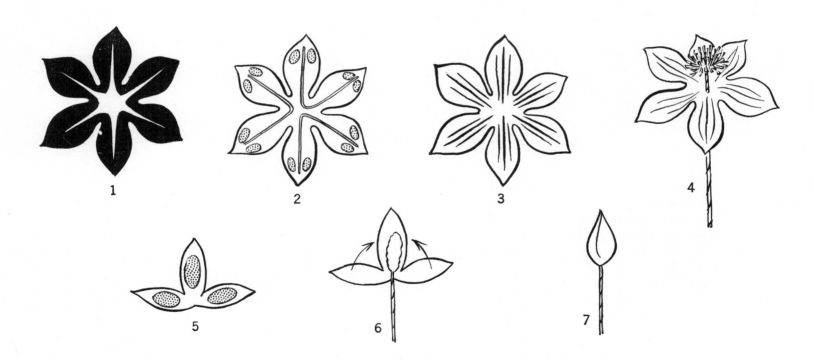

HYDRANGEA

MATERIALS (*for one head of flowers and ten leaves*)

Flowers: Thin cotton of a suitable shade of blue, pink, or white. (If so desired, use velveteen or rayon velvet for some of the flowers to add volume to the cluster.)

Stamens: White cotton thread and white glue (see page 46). Make seventeen stamens, each 2 in. long, six of them having heads slightly larger than the others. Also required are wire (#24) and green paper-tape.

Leaves: Green velveteen, wire (#24), and green paper-tape.

Main stem: 1 ft. 6 in. wooden stick (1/5 in. diameter), and green velveteen.

According to the pattern on page 100, cut out six large, eight medium, and three small flowers. Also six large and four small leaves, as well as the stem fabric.

To curve the back of each of the flower's petals, press the heated handle of a knife on the points marked in illustration 1. Then turn the flowers round and press their centers with the heated tips of a fork to make a deep hollow.

Pierce the center of each flower with an awl, pass a stamen through the hole (using stamens with larger heads for the large flowers), and glue the head of the stamen to the flower (illustration 2).

Apply glue to green paper-tape and use the tape to wrap a piece of wire (#24), 5 in. long, onto the cotton thread below each flower.

Glue a piece of wire (#24), wrapped with green paper-tape, down the center of the back of each leaf, extending it 2 in. beyond the base of the leaf. Then, as shown in illustration 3, glue a V-shaped length of wire (#24), also wrapped with green paper-tape, over the central wire. On large leaves, this bent wire should be 4 in. long, on smaller ones an inch shorter.

Make veins (as shown in the pattern) with the blunt edge of a knife on both sides of each leaf.

Now bunch the stems of the seventeen flowers to form a rounded head. Insert the tip of the wooden main stem between the bunched flower stems. Apply glue along the back of the strip of stem fabric and wrap it spirally round the bottom of the flowers' stems and down the entire length of the wooden main stem, allowing for the addition of the leaves. These

should be arranged in pairs, one leaf opposite the other, with the smaller pairs nearest the top and the space between the other pairs progressively increased down the main stem (illustration 4).

Three completed hydrangeas are shown in the plate on page 24.

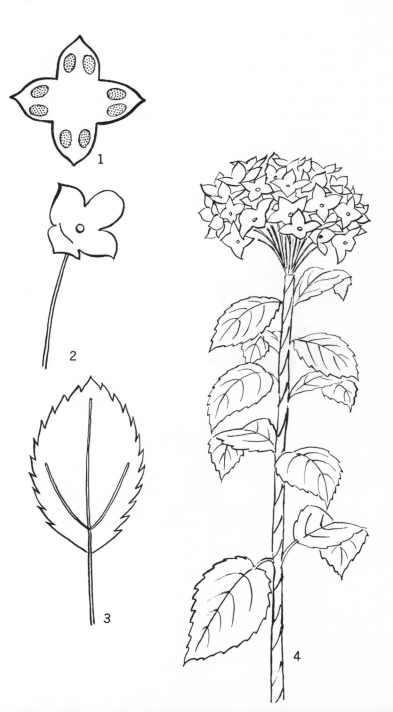

SUNFLOWER

MATERIALS (*for one flower and five leaves*)
Petals: Thin yellow cotton, wire (#24), and yellow paper-tape.
Stamens: Yellow rayon velvet.
Calyx: Green rayon velvet.
Leaves: Green rayon velvet or velveteen, wire (#24), and green
      paper-tape.
Upper stem: 1 ft. of wire (#20), and green paper-tape.
Main stem: Wooden stick (1 ft. 6 in. long and 1/3 in. in dia-
      meter) and green velveteen.

With the pattern on page 101 as a guide, cut out one set of petals, one strip of stamens (making slits as shown), one calyx, two small and three large leaves, and one strip of velveteen for the main stem.

Glue green paper-tape spirally round the upper stem's wire. Bend the tip of the wire and hang it in a slit at one end of the stamen fabric; then apply glue along the lower half of one side of the fabric and roll it up tightly. Now push the center of the roll slightly upward to produce the gently rounded effect shown in illustration 1.

Brush the tips of the stamens with brown poster color.

As shown in illustration 2, glue wire (#24), wrapped with yellow paper-tape, along the center of the back of each petal to within 1/2 in. of the top. Then, with a small heated knife, crease and curve the back of the petals as shown. Next make a row of running stitches 1/8 in. from the petals' base.

Gather the stitches and glue the lower part of the front of the petals round the rolled stamens (illustration 3).

Pierce the center of the calyx with an awl and pass the upper stem's wire through the hole so that the back of the calyx is inside. Stick the calyx onto the base of the flower.

Glue wire (#24), wrapped with green paper-tape, along the center of the back of each leaf, with the wire reaching 2 in. beyond the leaf's base. Over this wire, glue two other pieces of wrapped wire (#24), bent in a V-shape (illustration 4).

Make veins as shown in the pattern on both sides of the leaves.

Apply glue along the back of the stem fabric and use it to wrap the upper stem onto the wooden main stem. Winding the stem fabric down the rest of the main stem, add on the leaves. These should be arranged at intervals on alternate sides of the stem.

A bunch of sunflowers, their hearts made in a slightly different way, is shown on page 25.

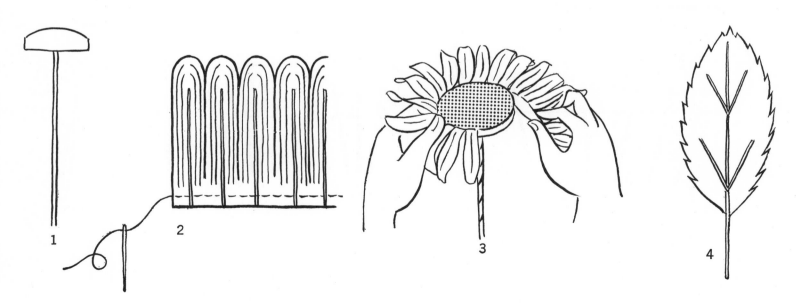

COCKSCOMB

MATERIALS (*for one flower and thirty-seven leaves*)
Crest: Red rayon velvet, wire (#24), and red paper-tape.
Flower's lower half: Red rayon velvet.
Seed vessels: Red rayon velvet.
Leaves: Green and cream-colored cotton, velveteen, or satin.
Also wire (#24), and paper-tape of the same color as the leaf fabric. (I recommend using two or three kinds of fabric and varying the color of the leaves.)
Main stem: Light green silk, and a wooden stick (1 ft. 8 in. long and 3/8 in. diameter).

First examine the color plate on page 26 for the form of this type of cockscomb—namely, a red, frilled crest with a cluster of tiny, pointed seed vessels immediately below it.

Then, working from the pattern on pages 102–104, cut out two large, twenty-four medium, and twelve small sections for the crest; two pieces of material for the lower half of the flower (cutting slits along the top as shown); one strip of rayon velvet for the seed vessels and one of silk for the main stem. For the leaves, cut out five As, five Bs, seven Cs, nine Ds, and eleven Es.

Prepare sixty pieces of wire (#24), each 4 in. long, by gluing red paper-tape spirally round each piece. Then, in the manner shown in illustrations 1, 2, and 3, stick six of these pieces onto the back of each of the crest's large sections, three pieces onto the back of each of twelve medium-sized sections, and two onto the back of each of six small ones. Fold both the large sections in half lengthwise to cover the wire's tips, and stick the two halves together.

Over each of the crest's medium and small sections that have wires attached to them, glue a section of corresponding size (the back of the fabric inside) to cover the wire. Then stretch the top edges of all sections with moistened fingers to make waves in the fabric. Fold the small sections in half breadthwise (illustration 4), make loose, double folds in the medium-sized ones (illustration 5), and three folds in the larger ones (illustration 6).

Divide the crest's sections into two bunches (one large, six medium, and three small sections in each bunch), making the bunches not round but slightly fan-shaped. Then glue absorbent cotton thinly round the entire length of the wire stems of each separate bunch.

With the slits uppermost, stick each piece of material for the flower's lower half round this absorbent cotton. Shave flat

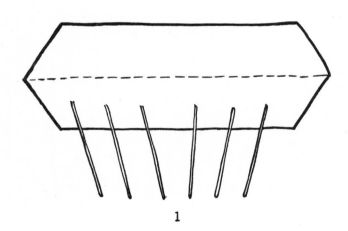

1

2

3

4

5

the end of the wooden main stem, place it between the two bunches, and tie the bunches tightly together with red thread at the base of the crest and just above the stem.

Now fold the material for the seed vessels in half to make a long, thick strip, and glue both halves together. Cut out small triangular pieces from it as shown in illustration 7, and stick them (pointing outward) round the joined lower halves of the flower (illustration 8).

Partly color the main stem fabric red with crayon or poster color (see the color plate). Apply glue to the back of it, and fold it lengthwise (not spirally) round the wooden stick.

Similarly, color parts of the leaves red or orange (see the color plate). Next glue wire (#24), wrapped with paper-tape of the same color color as the leaves, down the center of the back of each leaf, extending the wire 3–4 in. (depending on the size of the leaf) beyond the base. From the center to the base of the large leaves, a second piece of wrapped wire should be glued to the first as a support.

Make veins (as shown in the pattern) on both sides of each leaf with the blunt edge of a knife.

Now glue both the stem and the lower part of each leaf (1–2 in. according to the size of leaf) onto the main stem. The smaller leaves should be attached just below the flower, and the others spaced down the main stem with the largest at the bottom (illustration 9).

6

7

8

9

65

POINSETTIA

Materials (*for one bloom and eleven leaves*)
Flowers: White velveteen or thick cotton, wire (#24), and white paper-tape.
Gold and silver bracts: Lamé, wire (#24), and white paper-tape.
Gold and silver leaves: Same as for bracts.
Main stem: 8 in. of wire (#20), and white velveteen.

First, see the plate on page 27 for the form of the finished flower.

Then, working from the pattern on pages 104–105, cut out nine strips of flower fabric (making slits as shown); two silver and three gold bracts; one small and one medium-sized gold leaf; two small, two medium, and five large silver leaves; and a strip of stem fabric.

Glue white paper-tape spirally round each of nine pieces of wire (#24), each 3 in. long. Bend the tip of each piece of wire and hang it in a slit at one end of a strip of flower fabric. After applying glue along the lower inside edges of the flower fabrics, roll them up tightly and sprinkle the top of each roll with slivers of gold thread.

Down the center of the back of each leaf and bract, stick wire (#24) wrapped with white paper-tape, allowing it to extend 1–2 in. beyond the base of the leaf. Then, in the same way as for bougainvilleas and hydrangeas, glue another piece of wrapped wire (#24), bent in a V-shape, over this central wire.

With the blunt edge of a knife, make veins (as shown in the pattern) on both sides of the leaves and bracts.

Combine the nine flowers by wrapping their short stems together with white paper-tape, starting 2 in. below the top of the flowers. Then, at the same point, attach the bracts by wrapping spirally with one end of the stem fabric (glue applied to the back of it). As shown in the color plate, the bracts should be arranged in a star shape and grouped according to color.

Attach the main stem by winding the rest of the strip of stem fabric spirally round it, allowing for the leaf stems to be included at the same time. These should be added so that a the leaves, as seen from above, form the same star shape as the bracts. In addition, the lowest leaves should not be more than 4 in. below the bracts.

ROSE OF WHITE GAUZE

Materials (*for one flower and five leaves*)
Petals, stamens, and calyx: White gauze.
Leaves: White gauze, wire (#24), and white paper-tape.
Stem: 7 in. of wire (#24), 7 in. of plastic tube (1/8 in. in diameter), and white gauze.

Cut out, according to the pattern on pages 106–107, one of each of the sets of petals marked A, B, C, D, and five of the petals marked E. Also one strip of stamen fabric; five sections for the calyx; five leaves; and a strip of stem fabric.

Pass the stem wire through the plastic tube and loop the tip of the wire over the tube's rim. Then glue the strip of stem fabric spirally down the entire tube.

Fold the strip of stamen fabric in half lengthwise and cut thin slits in it from the folded edge to within 1/8 in. of the base (illustration 1). Then turn it inside out (without pressing flat the edge along which the slits have been cut) and stick the bottom of the two halves together. Now roll the strip of stamens, applying glue along the lower edge of one side, round the tip of the stem (illustration 2).

Fold two of the petals E in half lengthwise, and on each of the other petals E make a lengthwise fold of about one third of their width. With the heated handle of a knife, press the places shown in illustration 3 to curve each of these petals into a hollow. Now open them out.

Moisten the other sets of petals with a damp towel. Using the heated handle of a knife, make a dip in the center of each petal in set D (illustration 4). Then, with the same implement, press on the lower center of each petal C to make a deep dip, and curve the upper edges inward slightly. Now, on one side of each petal in set B, press on the places shown in illustration 5 as round, unshaded areas; turn the petals over and press on the parts shown as shaded areas. Then do the same with the set of petals A, using illustration 6 as a guide.

Glue along the lower inside edge of each petal E and stick the petals (with the curve outward) onto the base of the stamens; the tips of the petals should reach about 1/3 in. above the top of the stamens. Then make a hole in the center of the set of petals D, pass the stem through the hole, and glue the center to the bottom of the petals E, pressing the petals D up around the latter.

Now lay the remaining sets of petals one on top of the other with the set C uppermost and the set A on the bottom (arranging their petals to be alternately visible). Stick their centers together, pierce these with an awl, and pass the stem through the hole. Then glue the center of the upper set to the bottom of set D, and press the former's petals slightly upward.

Moisten the five sections for the calyx with a damp towel. Take each section and with the heated handle of a knife press on one side the part shown as an unshaded area in illustration 7; turn the sections over and press on the part shown as a shaded area (the result, sideview, should resemble illustration 8).

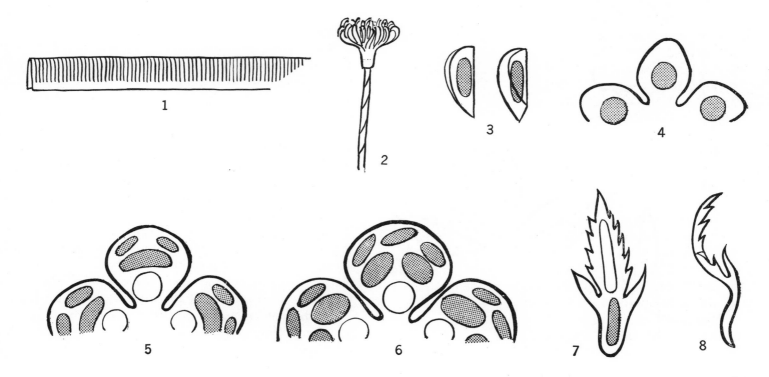

1

2

3

4

5

6

7

8

Leaving the upper part of each section free and curving outward, glue them to the bottom center of the flower in a star shape (illustration 9).

Then stick wire (#24), wrapped with paper-tape, down the center of the back of each leaf, extending the wire 1–2 in. beyond the base as a leafstalk.

Make veins (as shown in the pattern) on both sides of each leaf with an awl or the blunt edge of a knife. Then make two separate sets of leaves, one of three leaves, the other of two, by wrapping their stems together spirally with white paper-tape, applying glue along one side of it (illustration 10).

Finally, join the leaves to the flower's stem by wrapping with white wire or paper-tape.

The completed rose is shown in the color plate on page 28. Note that its stamens differ from those used here, being made of white cotton thread.

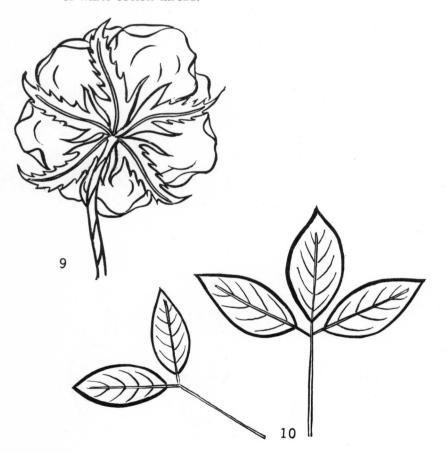

9

10

68

WILD ORCHID

MATERIALS (*for seven flowers and two buds*)
Flower petals: Mixed rayon velvet, satin, and cotton, with the predominant color pale blue but some petals white or cream-colored.
Bud petals: Blue rayon velvet, and absorbent cotton.
Stamens: White rayon velvet.
Stems: Thin, light green cotton, and wire (#24).

Working from the pattern on page 108, cut out eight sets of rayon velvet petals (two blue ones being used for the bud), six sets of satin petals, two sets of cotton ones, seven strips of stamen fabric (making slits as shown), and nine strips of stem fabric.

Cut wire (#24) into seven pieces, each 6 in. long, to serve as the flower's stems. Wrap each piece spirally with a strip of stem fabric, after applying glue along the back of the fabric. Bend the tip of each stem to hang in a slit at one end of each piece of stamen fabric; then apply glue along the lower edge of the back of each strip of stamens and roll the strip up evenly round the top of the wire. Color the tips of the stamens yellow.

Before going any further, form the sets of petals for the the seven flowers into the following combinations (bearing in mind that each flower is composed of two sets of petals): each of four of the flowers should combine one set of rayon velvet petals and one of satin; each of two flowers should be made with one set of rayon velvet petals and one of cotton; and the last flower should have two sets of satin petals.

Now curve each of the flowers' petals by pressing the heated handle of a knife on the points marked in illustration 1 (press the unshaded points on the front of the fabric, the shaded ones on the back).

Apply glue to the front lower edge of each flower's set of petals and stick one set onto the base of each roll of stamens. Then, keeping to the combinations of fabrics already specified, glue a second set of petals underneath the first, placing it so that the petals of each set are alternately visible (illustration 2).

For the buds' stem, cut off two pieces of wire (#24), each 7 in. long. Wrap each piece spirally with a strip of stem fabric (glue applied to the back of it). Glue a small oval-shaped ball of absorbent cotton round the tip of each of these stems. Then place one ball in the center of the back of each of the bud's two sets of petals (illustration 3), fold the petals upward round the absorbent cotton, and glue their edges together (illustration 4).

Finally, combine the flowers and buds by tying their stems together with a ribbon.

Compare your results with the example shown in the center of the plate on page 28.

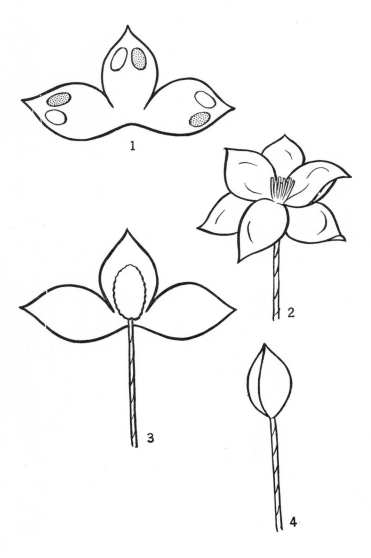

GREEN ROSE

MATERIALS (*for one flower, one bud, and five leaves*)
Flower petals: Light green rayon.
Bud: Same as above, and absorbent cotton.
Stamens: White or cream rayon velvet.
Calyxes: Green velveteen.
Leaves: Green velveteen, wire (#24), and green paper-tape.
Stems: Light green silk, 1 ft. 1 in. of plastic tube (1/8 in. in diameter), and 1 ft. 1 in. of wire (#24).

Using the pattern on pages 108–109, cut out nine large, eleven medium, and twelve small petals (three of the latter for the bud); one strip of stamen fabric; one large and four small leaves; two calyxes; and two strips of stem fabric. Cut a slit at the base of each petal as shown.

Cut each length of tube and wire for the stems into two pieces, 7 in. and 6 in. long; the longer pieces are for the bud, the shorter for the flower. Pass the wire through the tube and bend the wire's tip over the rim of the tube. Then wrap each tube with a strip of stem fabric, applying glue along the back of the fabric.

Fold the strip of stamen fabric in half lengthwise, with the front of the fabric inside. Cut thin, vertical slits along the folded edge to within 1/8 in. of the bottom. Then open it out and fold it again with the front outside, sticking the bottom of the two halves together.

Apply glue along the lower edge of one side of the folded stamens and roll it up around the tip of the shorter stem. On the tip of the longer stem, glue a small oval-shaped ball of absorbent cotton (the heart of the bud).

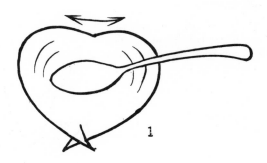

After moistening each petal slightly, make it curved by pressing the back of a small, heated spoon across the center of one side (illustration 1). This will be the inner side. Then take the two flaps of the slit base of each petal, cross them over each other, and glue them together.

Apply glue to the lower edges of the nine small petals for the flower, stick three of the petals onto the lower part of the rolled stamens, and add the others alternately around these three. The method of arranging them is shown in illustration 2.

After dyeing a strip of absorbent cotton light green, glue it thinly (so as not to open subsequent petals too much) round the base of the outermost small petals. Then apply glue to the lower inside edge of each medium and large petal and add them round the smaller ones in the way explained in illustration 2. The results should resemble illustration 3.

On the back of each calyx, press the points marked as shaded areas in illustration 4 with the heated handle of a knife. Then paste one calyx (with the back inside) round the base of the flower; this is most easily done by turning the flower upside down.

For the bud, apply glue along the edges of the three remaining small petals and completely enfold the longer stem's ball of absorbent cotton with one of them (illustration 5). Attach the other two more loosely, as shown in illustration 6. Now stick the main body of the second calyx (with the back inside) round the top of the stem, so that the arms of the calyx reach up round the base of the bud (illustration 7).

Pinch the neck of each calyx with wire to swell their bases (see color plate 14 on page 11).

Stick wire (#24), wrapped with green paper-tape, down the center of the back of each leaf, extending it about 1 1/2 in. beyond the base of the leaf. Then make veins (as shown in the pattern) on both sides of each leaf with a knife or awl. Make two separate sets of leaves, one of three leaves (the large leaf placed centrally), the other of two, by wrapping their stems together with a strip of stem fabric (glue applied to one side of the fabric).

Join the stems of the bud, flower, and leaves together with a ribbon.

A completed green rose is shown in the plate on page 28.

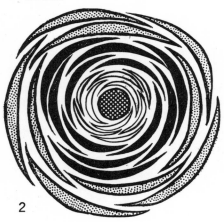
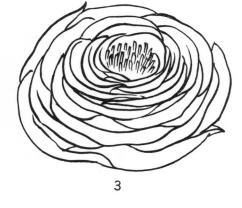

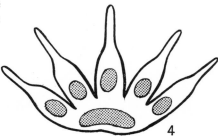

9 large petals (lightly shaded); 11 medium petals (black); 12 small petals (unshaded). The dotted area at the center of the illustration represents the stamens.

70

CAMELLIA

MATERIALS (*for one flower, one bud, and three leaves*)
Flower petals: Red velveteen, wire (#24), and red paper-tape.
Bud: Red velveteen.
Stamens: Yellow rayon velvet.
Calyxes: Light green rayon velvet.
Leaves: Green rayon velvet or velveteen, wire (#24), and green paper-tape.
Stems: Light green rayon velvet or cotton, wire (#24), and absorbent cotton.

Using the pattern on page 110, cut out three large, three medium, and six small petals (three of the latter being used for the bud); one strip of stamen material; two large and two small calyxes; one small and two large leaves; and two strips of stem fabric.

Moisten the stamen material slightly, and with the points of a fork make close, vertical lines along the back of the material, on all but the upper third of it. Then cut slits, 5/8 in. long, along the top edge, and stretch the material just below the slits with moistened fingers.

Wrap together three pieces of wire (#24), each 6 in. long, with a strip of stem fabric, after applying glue along the back of it. Then wrap absorbent cotton round the tip of this stem in a cocoon shape about 3/8 in. long. Apply glue along the lower part of the stamen material and roll it round the absorbent cotton; then, with your fingers, squeeze in the material slightly at a point about one third up from the base (illustration 1).

Moisten the petals with a damp towel. With the heated handle of a knife, press the center of the back of each small petal (the shaded area in illustration 2). Then make a shallow dip on the lower center of the face of each medium and large petal, and stretch their upper part to make waves in the fabric (illustration 3). Stick wire (#24), wrapped with red paper-tape, on the back of each petal from the center to the base, extending the wire about 1/3 in. beyond the base.

Next, apply glue along the lower inside edges of all but three of the small petals (the three are for the bud), and fold them round the stamens with their side edges overlapping (illustration 4). Then stick the bases of the medium petals round the small ones, and add the large petals, with edges overlapping alternately, round the medium ones (see illustration 6 overleaf. Note that the large petals are quite open).

On the back of one large and one small calyx, press the places shown in illustration 5 with the heated handle of a knife. Wrap a thin strip of absorbent cotton round the base of the flower. Pierce these calyxes' centers (with the smaller calyx uppermost and the back of the fabric inside), and glue them to the base of the flower so that the edges of the smaller calyx are alternately visible (see illustration 6).

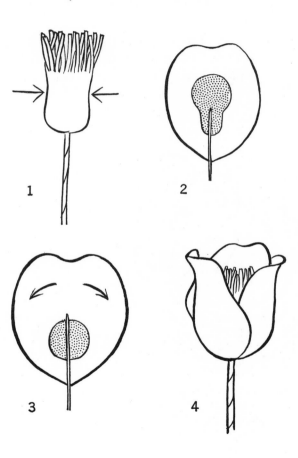

1

2

3

4

For the bud, glue a strip of a stem fabric (with the back inside) spirally round the upper part of three pieces of wire (#24), each 8 in. long, leaving the rest bare until the flower and leaf stems are added. Stick a small oval-shaped ball of absorbent cotton onto the tip of the stem. Next apply glue to the base and lower edges of the bud's three small petals and fold them round the absorbent cotton. Paste the remaining two calyxes, arranged in the same way as for the flower, onto the base of the bud (illustration 7).

Down the center of the back of each leaf, paste wire, wrapped with green paper-tape, extending it 1–2 in. beyond the base of the leaf.

Wrap the stems of the flower and leaves onto the bud's stem with the rest of the stem fabric (glue along its back).

The color plate on page 29 gives an example of completed camellias.

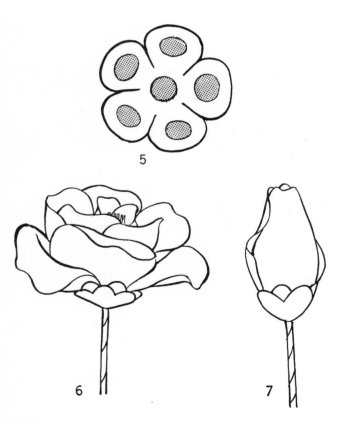

WHITE SWAN ROSE

MATERIALS (*for one flower and five leaves*)
Petals: White rayon.
Calyx: Green velveteen.
Leaves: Green velveteen, wire (#24), and green paper-tape.
Stem: Thin, light green silk, 7 in. of plastic tube (1/8 in. diameter), and 7 in. of wire (#24).

According to the pattern on pages 111–112, cut out six large, six medium, and seven small petals, one large and four small leaves, one calyx, and a strip of stem fabric.

On one side of each small petal, lightly shade the lower part pale green with a crayon. This will be their outer side. On the same side, color the central area of only one of these petals with a pink crayon (see the example in the color plate on page 29). Also using a pink crayon, very lightly shade in the lower half of both sides of each medium and large petal.

Moisten all the petals slightly. Next lay two or three of the small ones together at a time, and press on the center of their inner sides with the heated handle of a knife to curve them into a hollow (illustration 1). Repeat this process with three of the medium-sized petals. Then take the other medium-sized ones and using the heated knife-handle, press on their inner sides the part shown as an unshaded circle in illustration 2; turn the petals over, and press each on the places shown as shaded areas. Next, with a heated knife-handle or the back of a teaspoon, curve what will be the inner sides of the large petals into a hollow by pressing on the place shown as an unshaded circle in illustration 3; turn each large petal over, press on the part shown in the same illustration as a shaded area, and on this same side curl the top and side edges inward.

Now pass the stem wire through the plastic tube, and bend the tip of the wire over the tube's rim. Apply glue along the back of the strip of stem fabric and wind it spirally round the upper part of the tube, leaving the rest bare until the leaves are added. Then glue an oval-shaped ball of absorbent cotton round the tip of the tube.

Apply glue to the bottom and side edges of one of the small petals (on its inner side) and fold it completely round the ball of absorbent cotton. Then apply glue along the same parts of three other small petals (leaving out the one shaded pink), and fold each in turn round the heart of the flower; as shown in illustration 4, these petals should be wrapped a little more tightly at the top than at the base.

Lay the remaining small petals one on top of the other, with the pink-shaded petal uppermost. Curl their upper right-hand edges outward and slide the upper two petals sideways slightly (illustration 5). Then stick their bases together. Take the three medium-sized petals that have been curved on one side only, and also place them one on top of the other; curl their right-hand side edges outward and stick their bases together (illustration 6).

Using illustration 7 and the color plate as guides, apply glue along the bottom inside edge of both these sets of joined petals, and attach each to the base of the inner flower; as illustrated, the left-hand sides of both sets should curl in around the inner flower.

Take two large petals and one of the remaining medium-sized ones. On the latter's inner side (the front of the fabric), curl the top edge outward to take up about half the petal's length, and also make a short, tight curl on both side edges. With each of the two large petals, increase the curl already made on the top edge so that it also takes up about half the petal's length. Then stick the bottom inside edge of each large petal to the bottom of the medium one's outer side, arranging the large petals to slant diagonally across it (illustration 8).

In the same way, combine the other large and medium petals into two more sets; the medium petals, however, should be rather less curled than in the first set, and the large petals need not be curled any more than they have already been.

Stick the first set, applying glue along the bottom inside edge of the medium-sized petal, to the front left of the small, pink-sided petal already in place. Then, as shown in illustration

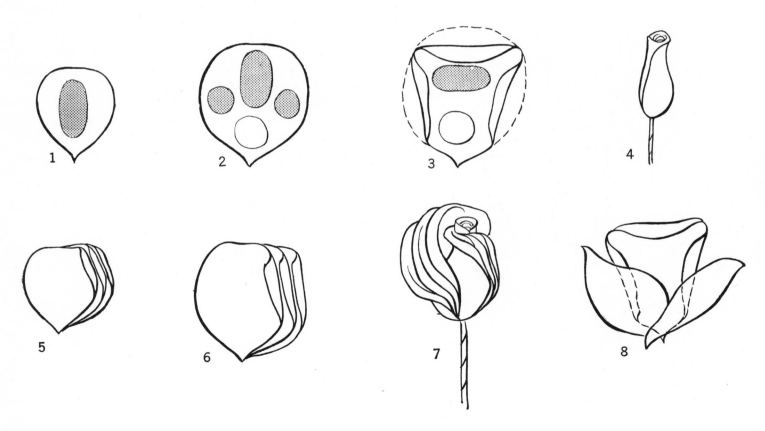

1 2 3 4

5 6 7 8

9 and the color plate, stick one of the remaining sets to the front right of the pink petal, in such a way that this set's medium petal crosses underneath the one in the first set. Glue the last set at the back of the flower.

Stick the calyx (with the back inside) round the base of the flower. Glue wire (#24), wrapped with green paper-tape, down the center of the back of each leaf, extending the wire 1–2 in. beyond the base. Make veins, as shown in the pattern, on both sides of each leaf.

As with the rose of white gauze, make two separate sets of leaves (one of three leaves, the other of two) by wrapping their stems together with green paper-tape, applying glue along one side of the tape.

Finally, join the leaves to the flower's stem with the rest of the strip of stem fabric.

The finished flower is shown on page 29.

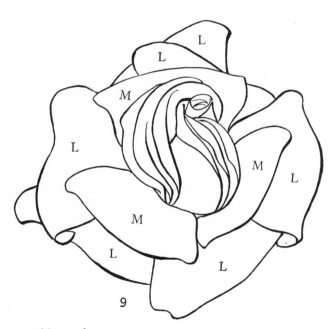

M = medium
L = large

BLACK ROSE

MATERIALS (*for one rose and three* leaves)
Petals, base, and calyx: Black georgette.
Leaves: Black velveteen, wire (#24), and black paper-tape.

Following the pattern on pages 112–113, cut out three large, three medium, and four small petals; one calyx and one base (the circular part onto which the petals are to be glued); one large and two small leaves.

Fold each petal in half lengthwise (illustration 1). Make a row of running stitches 1/5 in. from the base of each folded petal (illustration 2). Then draw the thread to gather the stitches, making the stitched edge on the large petals 4 in. wide, on the medium-sized ones 3 in. wide, and on each small one 2 in. wide.

Apply glue along the stitched edge of each petal. Take the large petals and stick their stitched edges flat onto the rim of the circular base, arranging these petals according to illustration 3. Then, placed according to the same illustration, attach the medium-sized petals, followed by three of the small ones, in the same way. At the heart of the flower, add the last small petal, folded into a budlike shape.

Glue the calyx flat onto the circular base.

Then stick wire (#24), wrapped with black paper-tape, down the center of the back of each leaf, and make veins (as shown in the pattern) on both sides of the leaves. Next glue the leaves, the large one placed centrally, onto the bottom of the calyx in the manner shown in illustration 4.

The color plate on page 29 gives an example of how the finished rose should look.

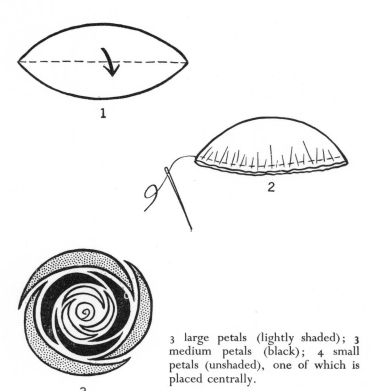

1

2

3 large petals (lightly shaded); 3 medium petals (black); 4 small petals (unshaded), one of which is placed centrally.

3

4

ARUM LILY

MATERIALS (*for one flower, one bud, and three leaves*)
Spathes (large bracts): White velveteen.
Spadices (fleshy spikes in center of flowers): Absorbent cotton.
Leaves: Green velveteen, wire (#22), and green paper-tape.
Stems: Wire (#22), plastic tube (1/8 in. in diameter), and thin light green silk.

Working from the pattern on page 114, cut out one large, one medium, and one small leaf; two spathes (one for the flower, the other for the bud); and five strips of stem fabric (making the one for the bud 2 in. longer than the others).

For the flower's stem, cut off 10 in. of wire and the same of plastic tubing. Pass the wire through the tube, then bend the tip of the wire and loop it over the rim of the tube. Glue a strip of stem fabric spirally round the tube.

Make the bud's stem in the same way, but use the longer strip of stem fabric and 11 in. of wire and plastic tube.

To form the spadices of flower and bud, wrap the ends of both stems with absorbent cotton, 1/4 in. thick and 2 in. long (illustration 1). Then color the absorbent cotton yellow with either felt pen or poster color.

With a light green crayon, delicately shade in the lower half of the front of the flower's spathe, making the shading darker

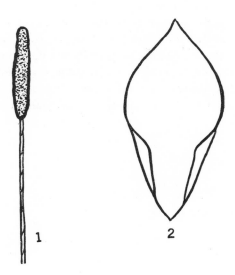

1

2

at the base than at the center. Then, on the same side, curl the lower edges inward about 1/8 in. with moistened fingertips (see illustration 2). This will be the spathe's inner side.

Twist the top of this spathe to make a fold in the fabric. Then glue the bottom of its inner side to the base of one spadix, and fold its lower quarter into a funnel shape round the spadix, sticking the funnel's edges together (illustration 3).

The bud is formed in much the same way. First twist the top edge of its spathe to make a gentle fold; then glue the bottom of its inner side (the front of the fabric) to the base of the remaining spadix. Finally, fold about two-thirds of the spathe into a narrow funnel shape, sticking down its edges (illustration 4).

Down the center of the back of each leaf, glue wire (#22) wrapped with green paper-tape, extending the wire 8 in. beyond the base of the leaf. Then on the large and medium-sized leaves stick another wrapped piece of wire, bent into a V-shape, across this central wire (as for hydrangeas and bougainvilleas).

On both sides of each leaf make veins as shown in the pattern.

Cut off three 8 in. lengths of plastic tube to serve as stems for the leaves. Pass the wire attached to each leaf through the tubes, bending the end of the wire over the bottom of the tubes. Then wrap a strip of stem fabric spirally round each tube.

To make a bunch of arums like that shown in the top left of the plate on page 30, merely tie the stems of the flower, bud, and leaves together with a ribbon. For the arums in the larger photograph, the scale of the pattern should be proportionately increased, the stems being wooden sticks wrapped with velveteen and the leaves made of green PVC. (The mural, incidentally, is of the Alhambra garden in Granada.)

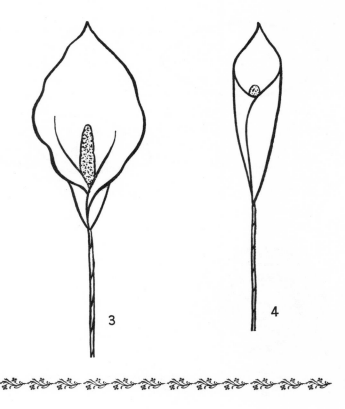

CANNA

MATERIALS (*for two flowers, one bud, and three leaves*)
Flower petals: Red or yellow rayon velvet, paper-tape of same color, and wire (#22).
Bud petal: Same as above, and absorbent cotton.
Stamens: Cream-colored rayon velvet.
Calyxes: Light green rayon velvet.
Leaves: Reddish brown rayon velvet for red flowers, green rayon velvet for yellow ones. Also paper-tape of same color, and wire (#22).
Main stem: Red or yellow rayon velvet, and 1 ft. of wire (#20).

With the pattern on pages 115–117 as a guide, cut out two sets of large petals and two sets of smaller ones; one petal for the bud; two sets of stamens (making slits as shown), three calyxes, one large and two small leaves; and a strip of stem fabric.

Wrap two 6 in. pieces of wire (#22) spirally with paper-tape, glued along one side. Bend the tip of each wire and hang it in a slit at one end of each strip of stamens; then, applying glue to the lower inside edge of the stamen fabric, roll it up evenly round the wire. Spread out the stamens slightly.

Now glue another piece of wire, wrapped round with paper-tape (red or yellow, depending on the petal's color), onto the center of the back of each set's petals (except the bud's), running from the base to within a short distance of the petals' tips (illustration 1). Then, on the front of the petals, make a central vein from base to tip with the blunt edge of a knife.

To produce waves on the petals' edges, twist them with moistened fingers. Then apply glue along the bottom edge of the front of the sets of small petals, and fold each small set round a roll of stamens. Below this smaller set, attach a large one, applying glue along its bottom inside edge. The larger petals should be placed so as to appear alternately between the smaller ones (illustration 2). Finally, curve each of the flowers' petals outward with moistened fingers.

In an even spiral round the stem below each flower, glue a strip of paper-tape (red or yellow according to the flower's color). Then glue absorbent cotton thinly round both the top of the stem and the lower part of the flower, and paste a calyx (with the back inside) over it.

Wrap paper-tape of an appropriate color round 4 in. of wire (#22) to serve as the bud's stem. Wrap the tip of the wire with an oval-shaped ball of absorbent cotton. Then place the latter on the center of the back of the bud's triangular petal in the way shown in illustration 3. Fold the petal's two halves over each other (illustration 4), apply glue along the lower inside edge, and pinch it in round the stem (illustration 5). Finally, paste a calyx (with the back inside) round the base of the bud.

Down the center of the back of each leaf, glue wire (#22), wrapped with paper-tape, extending the wire about 4 in. beyond the base of the leaf. Over this central wire, glue another wrapped piece, bent into a V-shape, in the same way as for hydrangeas (see page 62). To complete the leaves, make veins corresponding to those shown in the pattern on both sides of the leaves.

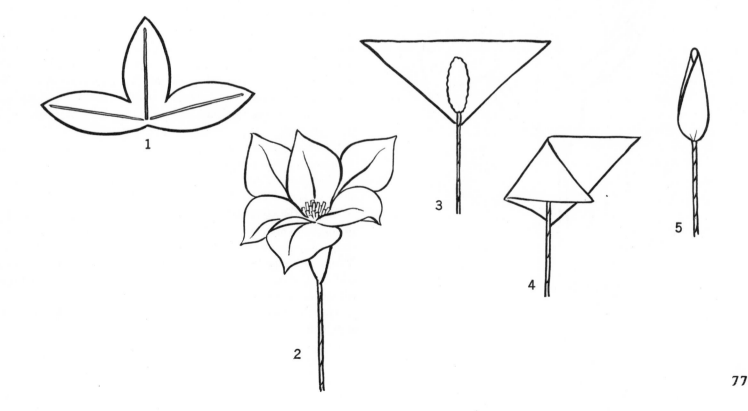

Join the bud's stem to the top of the main stem's wire by wrapping with the strip of stem fabric, applying glue along the back of the fabric. Winding the fabric down the rest of the stem, attach the stems of the flowers and leaves in the same arrangement as that shown in illustration 6.

Examples of completed cannas are shown in the plate on page 31. (The background is a scene from the Stadtpark in Vienna.)

6

CHINESE LANTERN PLANT

MATERIALS (*for five "lanterns" and three leaves*)
Bracts: Red velveteen, and wire (#24).
Leaves: Green velveteen, wire (#24), and pale green paper-tape.
Main stem: Pale green cotton, 2 ft. of wire (#20), and absorbent cotton.

Using the pattern on page 118, cut out one small, one medium, and three large sets of bracts; one small, one medium, and one large leaf; and a strip of fabric for the main stem.

Cut a length of wire (#24) into five pieces, three of them 3 in. long, the remainder 2 in. long. Glue light green paper-tape spirally round each piece of wire. Then bend their tips, and around each of them glue a small ball of absorbent cotton (illustration 1), making the ball slightly larger on the 3 in. stems.

Moisten lightly each set of bracts. With the blunt edge of a knife, make veins down the center of the back of each bract (illustration 2). This will be the bracts' inner side. Notice that the middle area of each set should not be veined.

Pierce the center of the inner side of each set of bracts, pass a stem through the hole (using the 3 in. stems for the largest bracts), and glue the middle of each set to the base of the absorbent cotton. Then close the bracts in each set round the absorbent cotton to form a lantern shape (illustrations 3 and 4), gluing their edges together and pinching along the joins with your fingertips.

Down the center of the back of each leaf, glue wire (#24) wrapped with green paper-tape, extending it 1–2 in. beyond the base of the leaf to serve as a stem. Make veins on both sides of each leaf as shown in the pattern.

Attach the stems of one small "lantern" and leaf to the top of the main stem by wrapping all three stems spirally with the strip of pale green cotton, after applying glue to the strip. When winding the cotton down the rest of the main stem, add on the other leaves and "lanterns"—the largest of these placed lowest down.

The color plate on page 32 shows how the finished flowers should look.

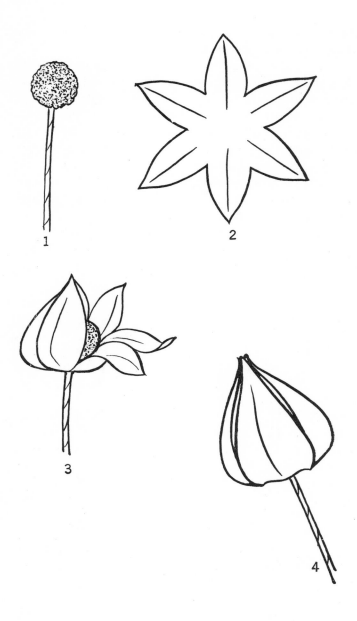

1

2

3

4

PINECONE

MATERIALS (*for one cone*)
Scales: Grayish brown velveteen.
Stem: 3 in. of wire (#24), and grayish brown paper-tape.

Cut out one strip of velveteen for the scales according to the pattern on page 119.

Fold the strip in half lengthwise, with the face of the material on the outside. Along the folded edge, cut slits, each 3/8 in. long, making the distance between the slits progressively shorter from left to right (at first 1/3 in., narrowing to 1/8 in.). Toward the top of each scale, make a dip by pressing the shaded areas shown in illustration 1 with the heated tips of a small fork.

Now wrap the stem spirally with the paper-tape, having applied glue to the back of the tape. Bend the tip (1/8 in.) of the wrapped wire, and glue absorbent cotton round it in the shape shown in illustration 2 (see overleaf).

On the same side as that on which the scales were made hollow, apply glue along the lower half of the strip of velveteen. Then, starting with the end that has the narrowest scales, wind the strip round the absorbent cotton from top to bottom, sliding each successive coil slightly downward (illustration 3) to produce the effect shown in illustration 4. Finally, twist the tip of each scale outward.

For a cluster of pinecones like that shown in the color plate on page 32, make a number of larger or smaller cones, altering the pattern's measurements accordingly. Then spray them with gold paint.

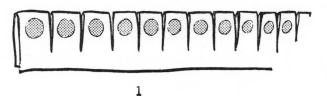

1

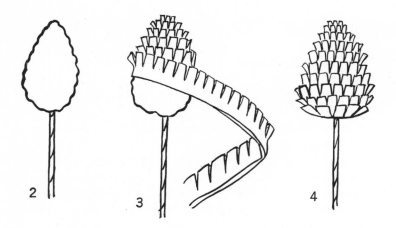

With moistened thumbs, press the center of one side of each petal to round. This will be their inner side.

Then apply glue along the lower inside edge of one small petal, fold the whole petal round the ball of absorbent cotton, and pinch in its base round the top of the stem (illustration 3).

Take the remaining two small petals and glue the bottom of their inner sides to the first petal, placing them facing each other on opposite sides of it (illustration 4). Then, being careful to keep the form of the rose fairly open, apply glue to the bottom of the medium-sized petals and arrange them alternately round the smaller ones. Finally, attach the five large petals in the same alternating pattern.

Pierce the center of the calyx with an awl, pass the stem through the hole, and stick the calyx to the base of the flower.

The finished flower is shown in the plate on page 33.

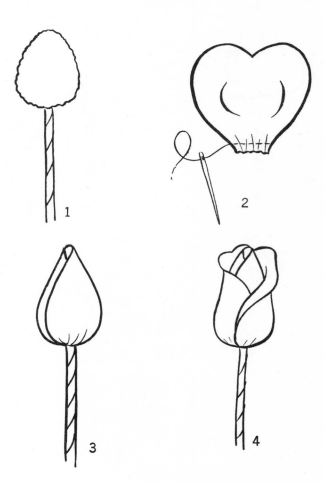

STRIPED ROSE

MATERIALS (*for one flower*)
Petals and calyx: Striped cotton.
Stem: Striped cotton, 6 in. of plastic tube (1/8 in. in diameter), and 6 in. of wire (#24). Also absorbent cotton.

Using the pattern on pages 119–120, cut out five large, three medium, and three small petals; one calyx; and a strip of stem fabric.

Pass the stem wire through the plastic tube, bend the wire's tip, and hook it over the rim of the tube. Glue a small, oval-shaped ball of absorbent cotton round the end of the tube, and wind the strip of stem fabric, with glue along one side, spirally down the whole stem (illustration 1).

Make a row of running stitches 1/8 in. from the bottom of each petal and gather about two-thirds of the base by pulling the thread (illustration 2).

FREE-PATTERNED FLOWERS

First select material of flowered design and starch the back of it.

Then, to make the larger specimens shown in the color plate on page 33, cut out two flowers of suitable size from the material; press the back of each of their petals with the heated handle of a knife to round; and, in the same way, press the center of the front of each flower to curve it into a hollow. To combine the two flowers, merely glue their edges together.

Alternatively, to make the sprig of smaller flowers featured in the same color plate, cut out a number of flowers and leaves of appropriate size. Curve the back of each petal and leaf by pressing them with the heated handle of a knife. Then press the center of the front of each flower to make a dip.

Cut off several pieces of thin wire to serve as stems and glue paper-tape of suitable color round each piece. Pierce the center of each flower, pass a stem through the hole, and hook the tip of the stem into the fabric. Also glue a stem up to the center of the back of each leaf.

Finally, join the stems of the flowers and leaves together by wrapping with white or colored ribbon.

ORIENTAL POPPY

MATERIALS (*for one flower*)
Petals: Red PVC.
Stamens: Black PVC.
Disk: Green cotton and absorbent cotton. (The disk is the round, flattened end of the stem.)
Calyx: Green cotton, 1 ft. of plastic tube (1/6 in. in diameter), and 1 ft. of wire (#22).

Cut out six petals (slitting the base of each), one disk, one strip of stamens (making slits as shown), one calyx, and a strip of stem fabric, according to the pattern on pages 120–121.

Pass the stem wire through the plastic tube and bend the tip of the wire over the tube's rim. Wrap the end of the tube with absorbent cotton in a small, flat shape (1/2 in. in diameter); then cover the absorbent cotton with the round disk fabric, apply glue to its inside lower edge, and pinch in its base round the stem (illustration 1). Round the disk, glue the strip of stamens (illustration 2).

To curve the front of each petal into a hollow, fold the two flaps at the base of each petal over each other and stick them together. Then twist the upper edges of the petals to make waves in the fabric.

Apply glue along the lower edges of the front of three petals and stick them to the bottom of the stamens. Around these petals glue the remaining three, arranging them so that the six petals alternate.

Pierce the center of the calyx, pass the stem through the hole, and stick the calyx onto the base of the flower.

A completed example of a red oriental poppy is featured in the plate on page 34.

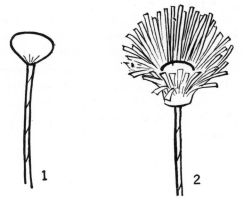

1   2

GOLD FLOWER

MATERIALS (*for one flower*)
Petals: Gold PVC.
Stamens: Gold PVC and black crepe paper.
Black trimmings (between large and small petals): Black crepe
    paper.
Stem: 1 ft. of wire (#22), and gray paper-tape.

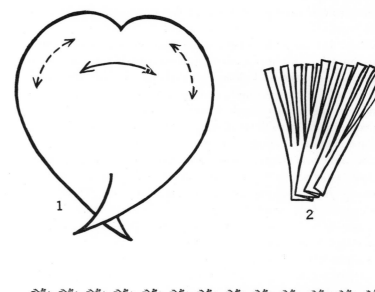

First, for reference to the form of this flower, see the color plate on page 34.

Then cut out, according to the pattern on pages 121–122, five large and three small petals; one strip of gold PVC stamens and a smaller one of black, crepe paper stamens; also three tall pieces of black crepe paper for the trimmings. As can be seen from the pattern, a single slit should be cut at the base of each petal, as well as slits along the top edge of the black stamens and trimmings. For the gold stamens, cut slits vertically from the top edge at increasing intervals from left to right, with intermediate slits along the middle of the fabric.

To make a shallow dip on the front of each petal, fold the two bottom flaps across each other and stick them together. Then stretch the upper parts of both sides of each petal in the directions shown in illustration 1 (the central arrow being for the front of the petal, the dotted ones for the back).

Now fold the stem wire in half and glue gray paper-tape spirally round it. Bend the tip of the wire and hang it in the slit at the left-hand end of the gold stamens; then apply glue to the bottom edge of the back of these stamens and roll them up from the left.

Apply glue along the base of the strip of crepe paper stamens and wrap it round the gold stamens. Then stick the bottom front of each small petal to the outer roll of stamens, spacing the petals evenly round the roll.

On the lower edge of each strip of trimming, make three tucks and glue the tucks together (illustration 2). Then glue each of these strips onto the bottom center of the front of three large petals. Apply glue along these large petals' lower front edges and add them round the smaller petals, placing them so as to appear alternately between these small ones.

Finally, attach the two other large petals on opposite sides of the flower.

CREPE PAPER ROSE

MATERIALS (*for one flower*)
Petals: Crepe paper of any suitable color.
Stem: 18 ft. of wire (#22), 6 ft. of plastic tube (1/6 **in.**
    diameter), and green paper-tape.

Cut out five large, three medium, and five small petals according to the pattern on page 123.

Cut the wire for the stem into nine pieces, each 2 ft. long. Cut the plastic tube in three. Then pass three pieces of the wire through each tube and bend their tips to hang over the tubes' rims. Wrap the three tubes together with green paper-tape, applying glue along one side of it. The stem is now complete.

To hollow the centers of the smallest petals, the lower centers of the medium-sized ones, and the large petals slightly nearer the base, use your fingers to press and stretch the appropriate places outward from the center line, as shown in illustration 1.

On the same side of each of the smallest and medium-sized petals, curl the top edge outward by rolling it over a pencil; gather the roll toward the center of the pencil (illustration 2); then remove the latter (illustration 3).

Curl the top and side edges of the large petals as shown in illustration 4.

Round the end of the stem glue a small ball of absorbent cotton. Apply glue to the bottom and side edges of the hollow side of one of the smallest petals, wrap the petal round the absorbent cotton, and stick its edges together, making the shape shown in illustration 5.

Then glue the lower inside edges of the remaining smaller petals around this first one, followed by the medium and large petals arranged in an alternating pattern.

Completed examples of this rose are featured in the plate on page 35.

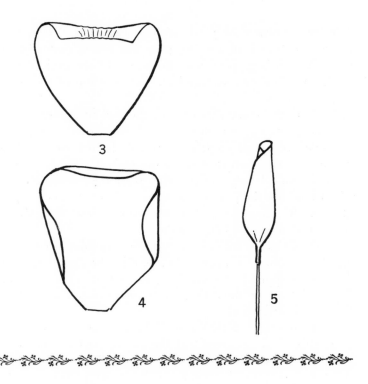

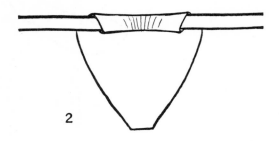

SMALL PINK ROSE

MATERIALS (*for one flower, one bud, and five leaves*)
Flower and bud petals: Thin pink silk or rayon.
Leaves: Green velveteen, wire (#24), and green paper-tape.
Calyxes: Green velveteen.
Stem: Green velveteen, 10 in. of wire (#24) for the flower, 1 ft. of wire (#24) for the bud, and absorbent cotton.

Cut out three large and five small petals for the flower, three small petals for the bud, one large and four small leaves, two calyxes, and two strips of stem fabric according to the pattern on page 124.

Fold the two stem wires in half and wrap each spirally with a strip of stem fabric, applying glue along the back of the fabric. Bend the tip (1/6 in.) of each stem and glue a small, oval-shaped ball of absorbent cotton round the tip (illustration 1 overleaf).

83

Slightly moisten the petals with a damp cloth. Then, with the heated handle of a knife, press the lower center of the front of each large petal and the center of the back of each small one (illustrations 2 and 3). Curl the top of the petals outward slightly.

To form the inner part of both the bud and flower, apply glue along the bottom edges of the back of two small petals, and fold each petal completely round the ball of absorbent cotton that caps each stem (illustration 4). Then apply glue to the base and side edges of the back of another small petal and add it opposite the join on the outside of the first petal. Apply glue to the same parts of a third small petal and fold it round the inner two (illustration 5).

The bud's petals are now in place. For the flower, however, attach two more small petals, followed by the three large ones (with glue applied only on the lower edges and base of the front side); these should be arranged alternately around the flower (illustration 6).

Glue absorbent cotton round the base of the flower and bud; this serves to swell out the calyxes, which should be glued (with the back inside) over the absorbent cotton. Then pinch the neck of each calyx by binding it with wire (see color plate 14 on page 11).

Stick wire, wrapped with green paper-tape, down the center of the back of each leaf, extending it about 1 1/2 in. beyond the base of the leaf.

By wrapping their stems together with green paper-tape, combine one large and two small leaves, and a pair of small leaves (as for the rose of white gauze, page 68).

Join the set of three leaves to the bud's stem, and the other leaves to the flower's stem, by wrapping with a strip of stem fabric (applying glue to the back of it).

A completed example of this rose is shown in the plate on page 36.

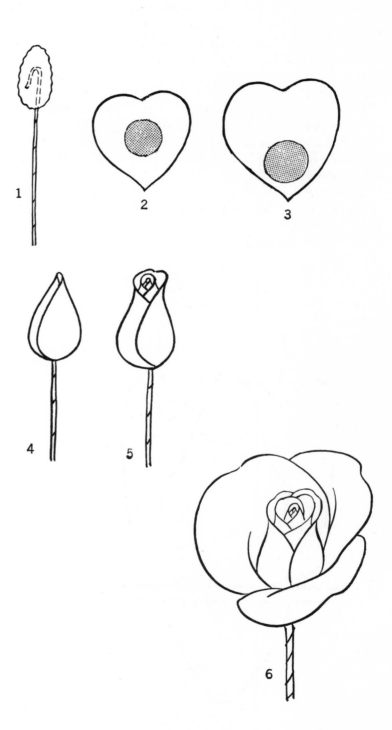

HEADBAND (Green roses)

MATERIALS
Petals: Thin, light green silk.

Keeping the plate on page 36 as a reference to the final form of this decoration, cut out forty petals according to the pattern on page 124. Then fold each petal in half lengthwise.

As shown in illustration 1, loosely coil each of seven petals into a slightly conical shape, with the folded edge uppermost, and stick down the end of the coil. Round each but two of these coiled petals, fold another petal, gluing one end to the inner coil and the other to the outside (illustration 2).

Crease each of the remaining petals in the following way: lay a petal in the center of a thin, moistened cloth and fold the cloth over it (illustration 3); then, pressing with one hand on the petal, draw the righthand edge of the cloth toward and under the pressing hand in a semicircle (illustrations 4 and 5). Finally, remove the petal and open it out.

One way of arranging the flowers and petals along the headband (which should be fairly broad) is to glue to it groups of four creased petals with a coiled flower pasted in the middle of them (illustration 6).

The other headbands shown in the same plate are made by using only creased (not coiled) petals in a flowerlike pattern.

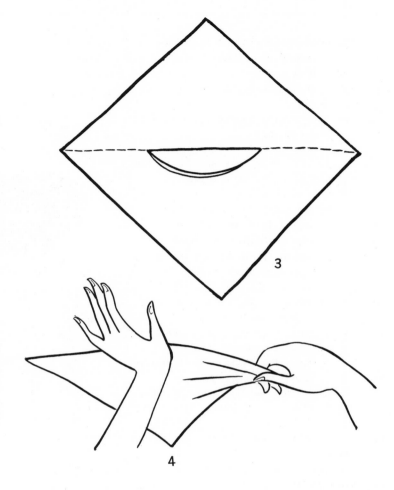

3

4

1   2

5   6

SPECIAL TOOLS AVAILABLE IN JAPAN
(department stores)

1. Foam rubber
2. Power handle with heating unit
3. Screwdriver
4. Socket wrench (for tightening nut on shaft of power handle)

INTERCHANGEABLE HEADS FOR POWER HANDLE
5. *Issun marugote* (1 1/6 in. in diameter)
6. *Hachibu marugote* (1 1/12 in. in diameter)
7. *Shichibu marugote* (1 in. in diameter)
8. *Gobu marugote* (3/5 in. in diameter)
9. *Sanbu marugote* (2/5 in. in diameter)
   These are used for making the larger sizes of petals hollow.

10. *Wasurenagusa-gote* (for hollowing small flowers like forget-me-nots)
11. *Futasuji-gote* (for making creases on flowers like chrysanthemums)
12. *Ben-gote* (large, for hollowing small flowers like violets)
13. *Hitosuji-gote* (for making creases on petals)
14. *Ben-gote* (small, for hollowing flowers like cherry blossoms)
15. *Suzuran-gote* (for hollowing the smallest of flowers)
16. *Suji-gote* (for making veins on leaves)
17. *Herikaeshi-gote* (for curling the edges of petals)

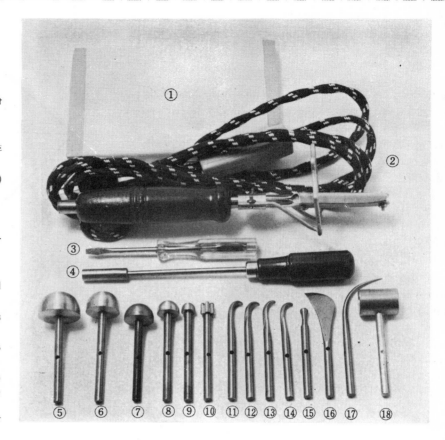

18. *Shakei-gote* (for rolling stem fabric into a tubular shape by passing it through the hole in the tool's head)

Patterns

ROSE *(The instructions for this flower are on pages 10–11)*

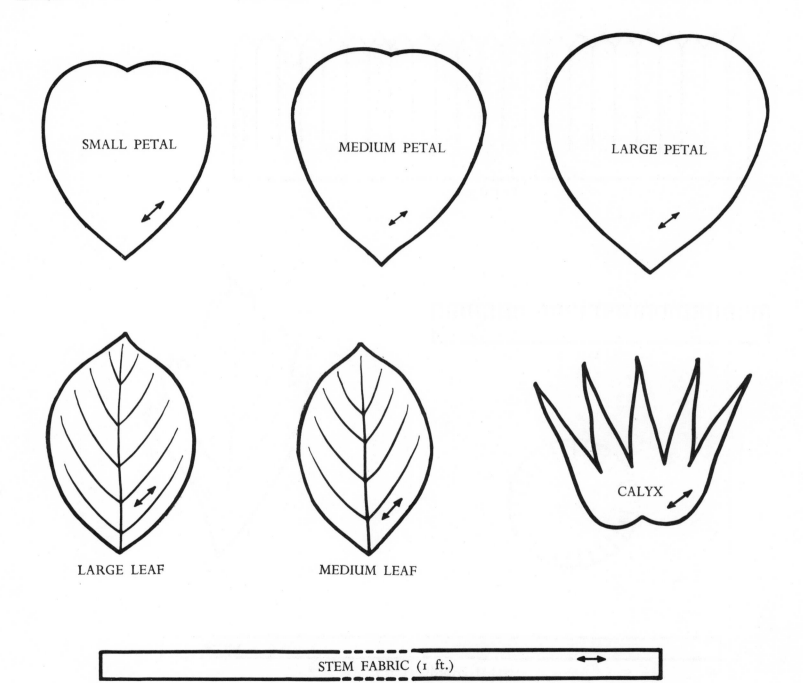

SMALL PETAL

MEDIUM PETAL

LARGE PETAL

LARGE LEAF

MEDIUM LEAF

CALYX

STEM FABRIC (1 ft.)

MARGUERITE

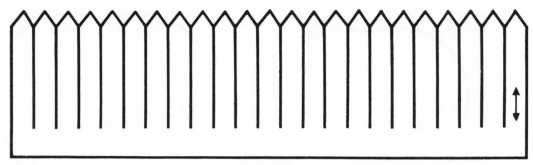

PETALS

STAMENS

CALYX

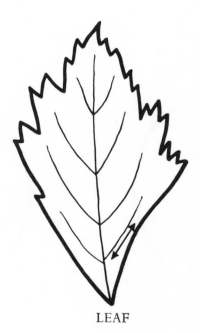

LEAF

STEM FABRIC (1 ft.)

BABY'S BREATH

FLOWER

PINK CARNATION

PETALS

CALYX

CORNFLOWER

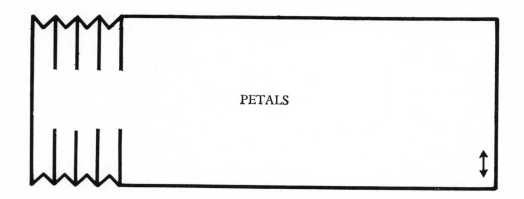

PETALS

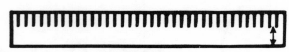

STAMENS

CALYX

FIELD POPPY

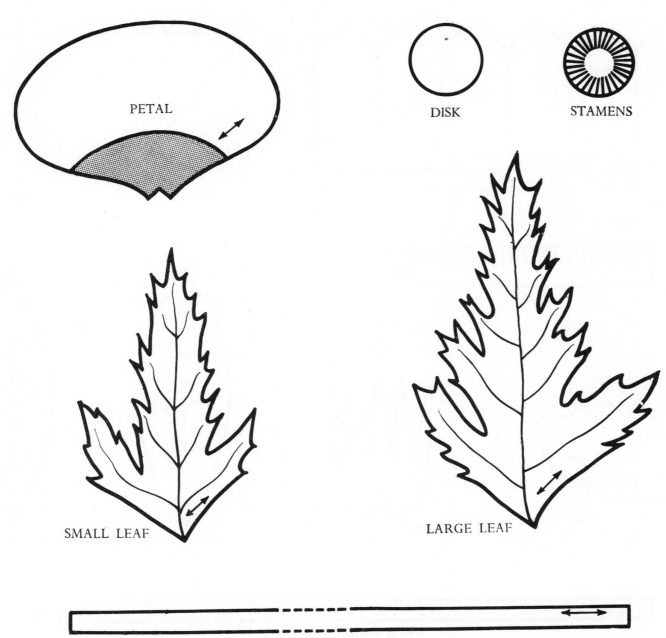

PETAL

DISK

STAMENS

SMALL LEAF

LARGE LEAF

STEM FABRIC (1 ft.)

CAPE JASMINE

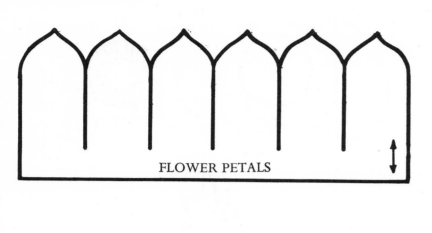

FLOWER PETALS

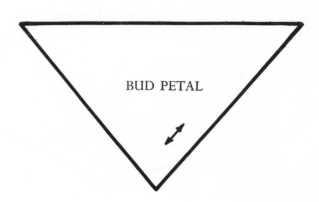

BUD PETAL

STAMENS

FLOWER CALYX

BUD CALYX

LARGE LEAF

SMALL LEAF

STEM FABRIC (10 in.)

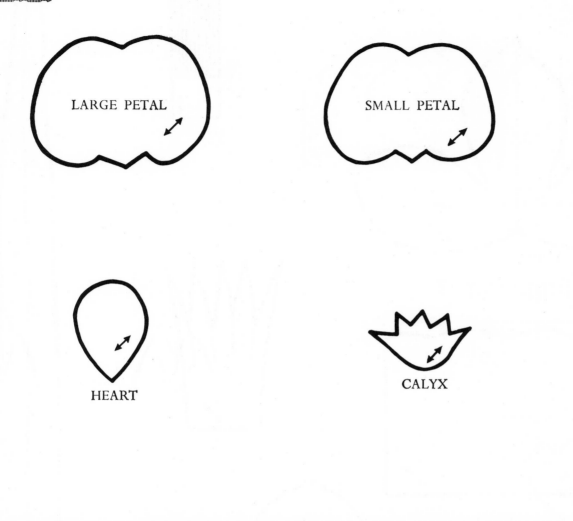

LARGE PETAL

SMALL PETAL

HEART

CALYX

STEM FABRIC (1 ft.)

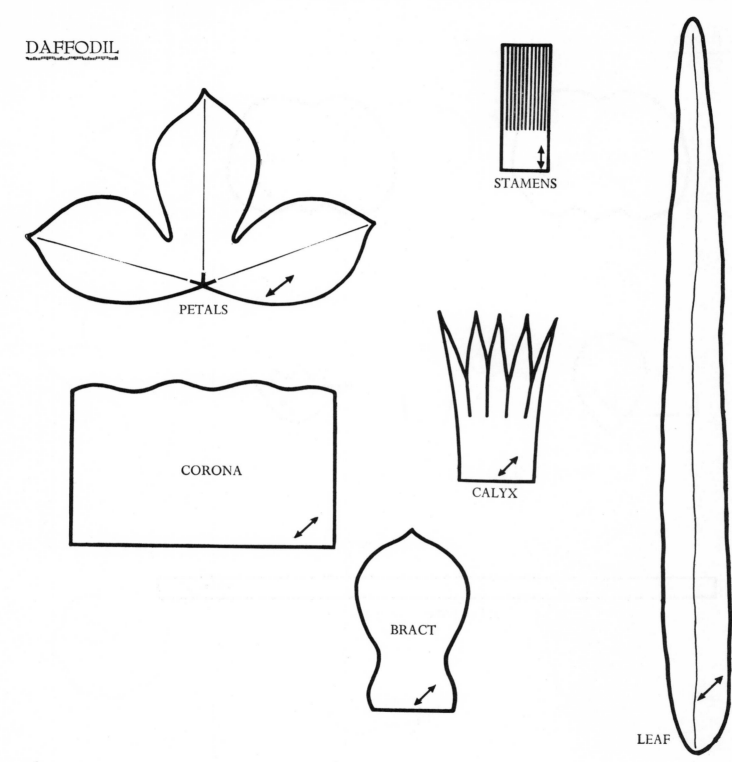

DAFFODIL

PETALS

STAMENS

CORONA

CALYX

BRACT

LEAF

NASTURTIUM

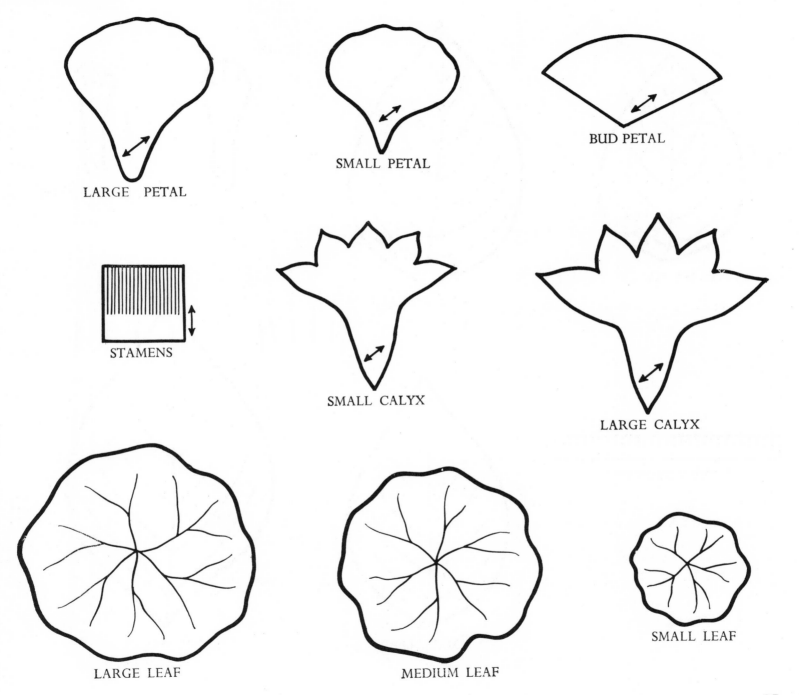

LARGE PETAL

SMALL PETAL

BUD PETAL

STAMENS

SMALL CALYX

LARGE CALYX

LARGE LEAF

MEDIUM LEAF

SMALL LEAF

BOUGAINVILLEA

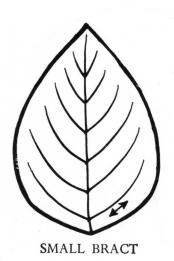

SMALL BRACT

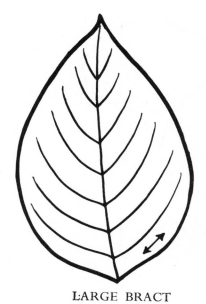

LARGE BRACT

LARGE CLOSED
FLOWER

SMALL CLOSED
FLOWER

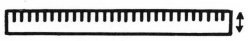

OPEN FLOWER

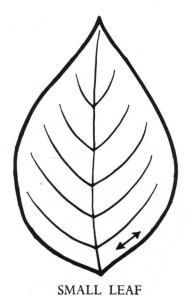

SMALL LEAF

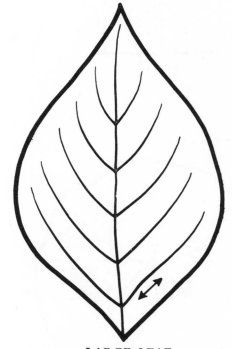

LARGE LEAF

98

CLEMATIS

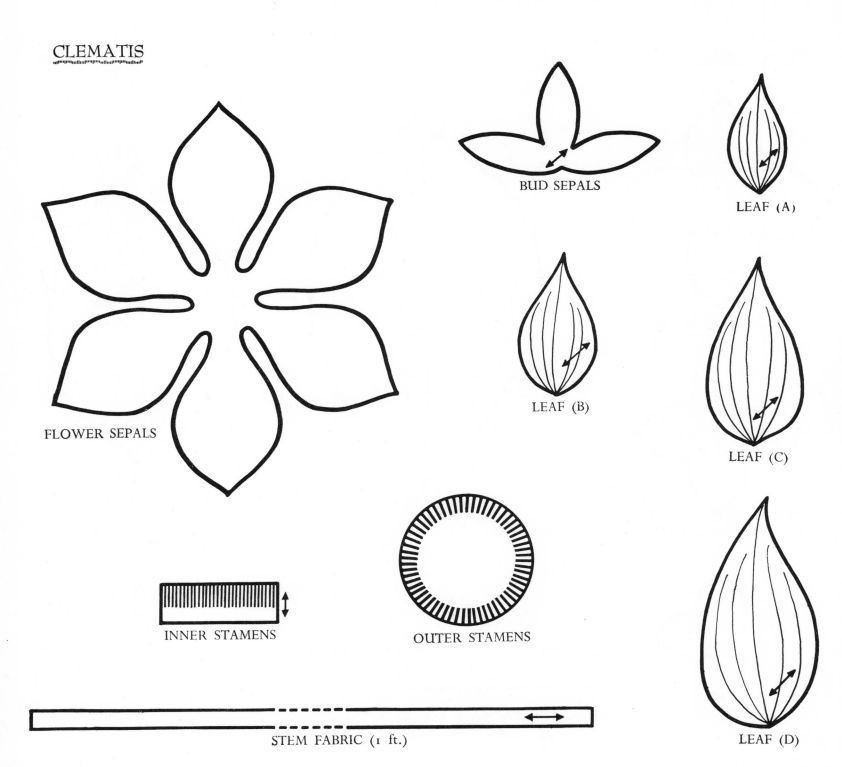

BUD SEPALS

LEAF (A)

LEAF (B)

LEAF (C)

FLOWER SEPALS

INNER STAMENS

OUTER STAMENS

STEM FABRIC (1 ft.)

LEAF (D)

HYDRANGEA

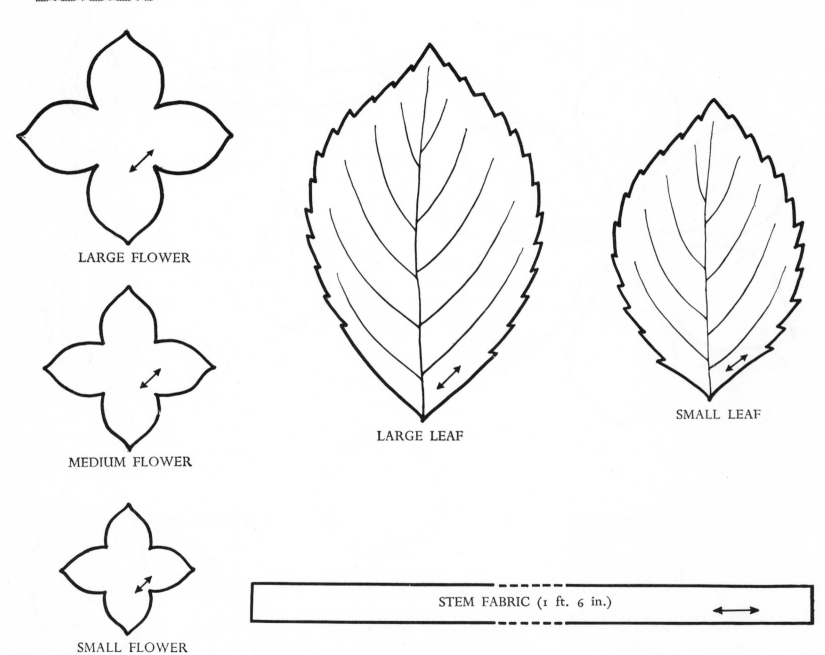

LARGE FLOWER

MEDIUM FLOWER

SMALL FLOWER

LARGE LEAF

SMALL LEAF

STEM FABRIC (1 ft. 6 in.)

SUNFLOWER

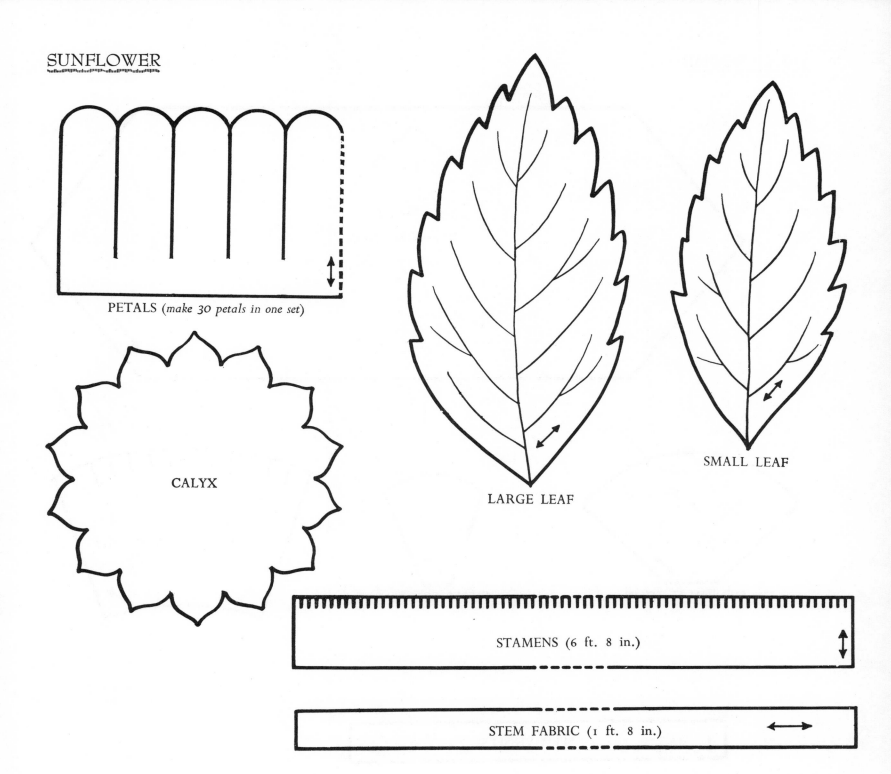

PETALS (*make 30 petals in one set*)

CALYX

LARGE LEAF

SMALL LEAF

STAMENS (6 ft. 8 in.)

STEM FABRIC (1 ft. 8 in.)

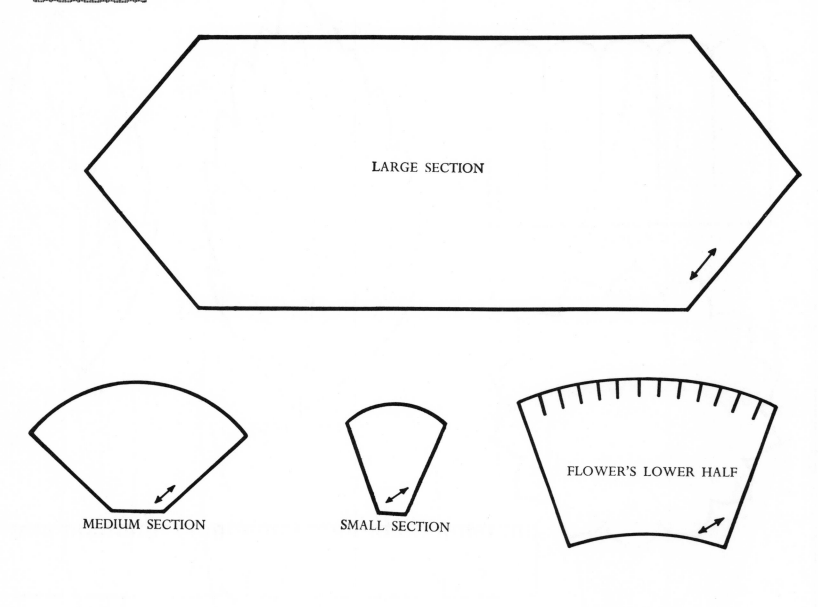

LARGE SECTION

MEDIUM SECTION

SMALL SECTION

FLOWER'S LOWER HALF

SEED VESSELS

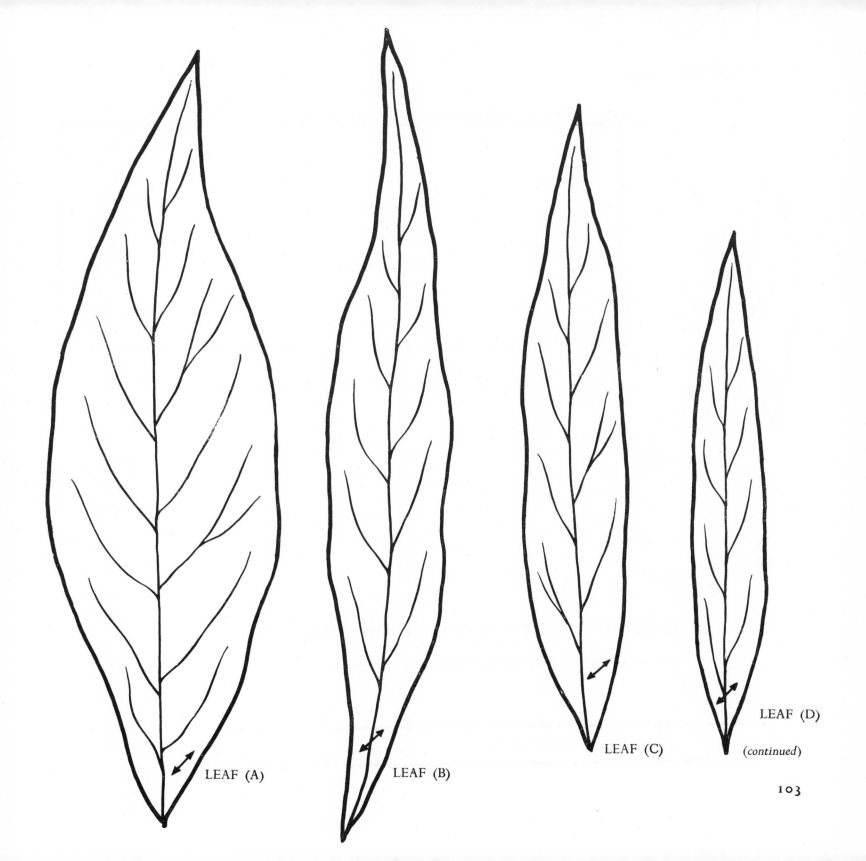

LEAF (A)

LEAF (B)

LEAF (C)

LEAF (D)

(continued)

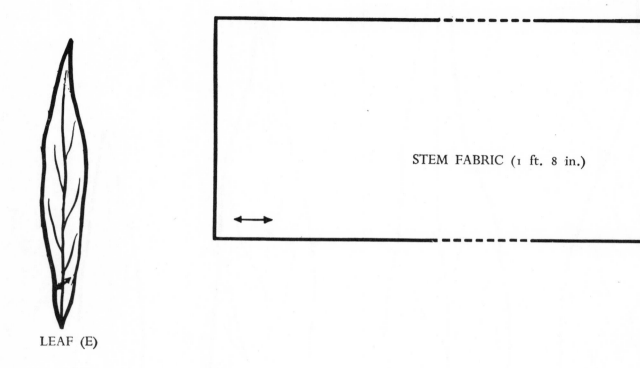

LEAF (E)

STEM FABRIC (1 ft. 8 in.)

POINSETTIA

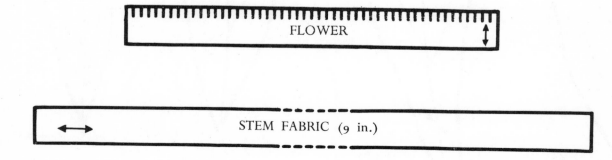

FLOWER

STEM FABRIC (9 in.)

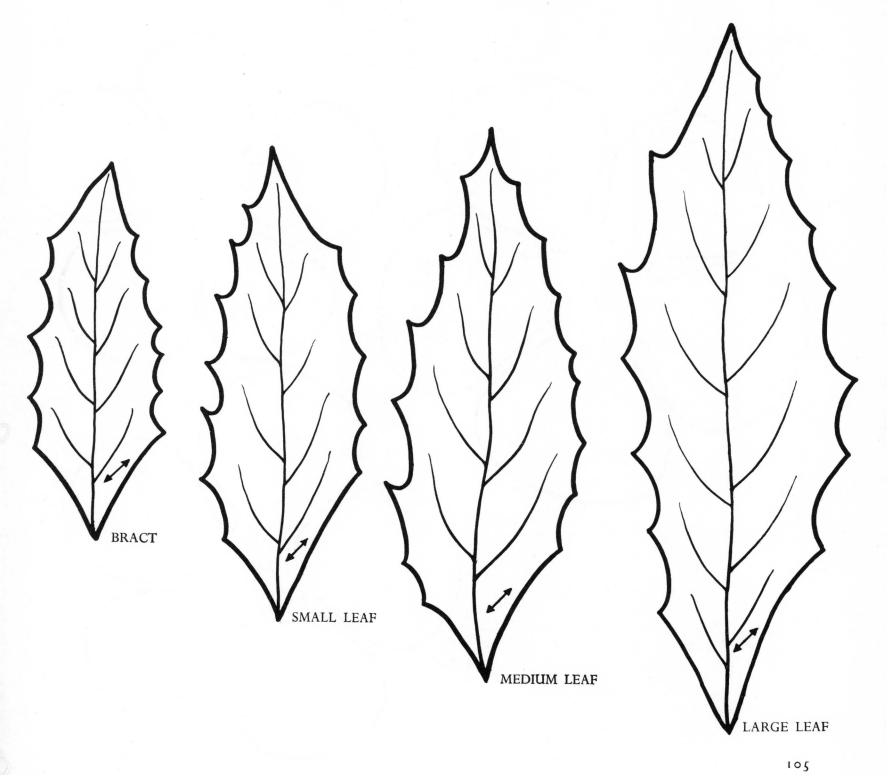

BRACT

SMALL LEAF

MEDIUM LEAF

LARGE LEAF

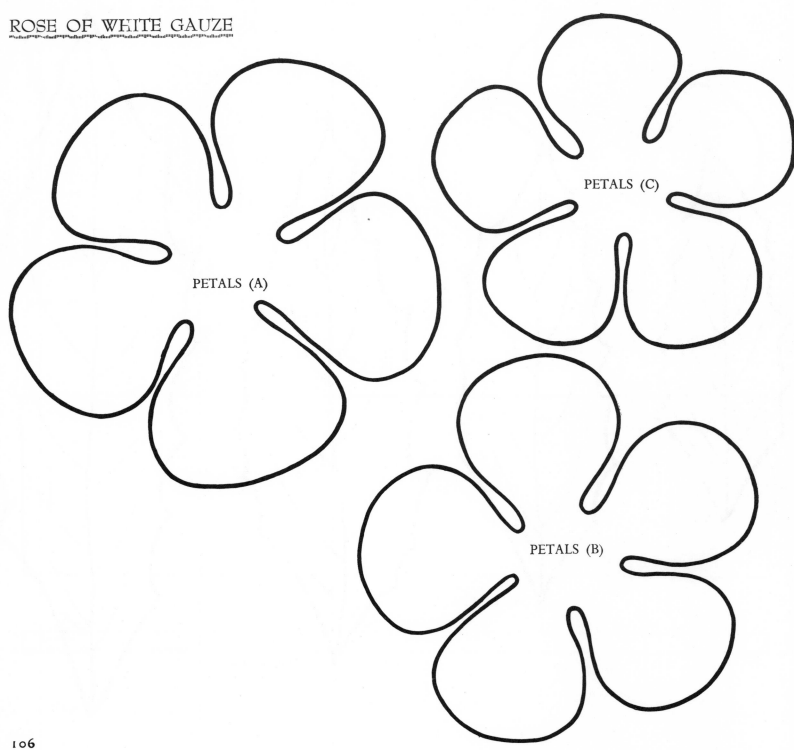

PETALS (C)

PETALS (A)

PETALS (B)

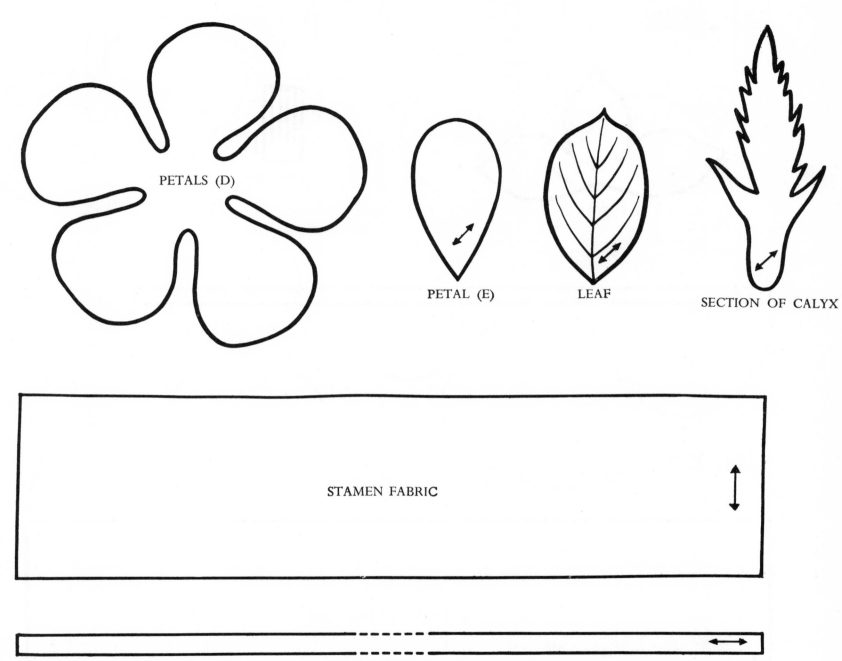

PETALS (D)

PETAL (E)

LEAF

SECTION OF CALYX

STAMEN FABRIC

STEM FABRIC (8 in.)

WILD ORCHID

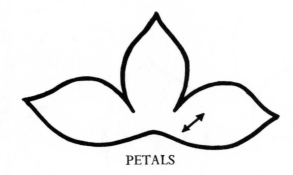

PETALS

STAMENS

STEM FABRIC

GREEN ROSE

STAMEN FABRIC

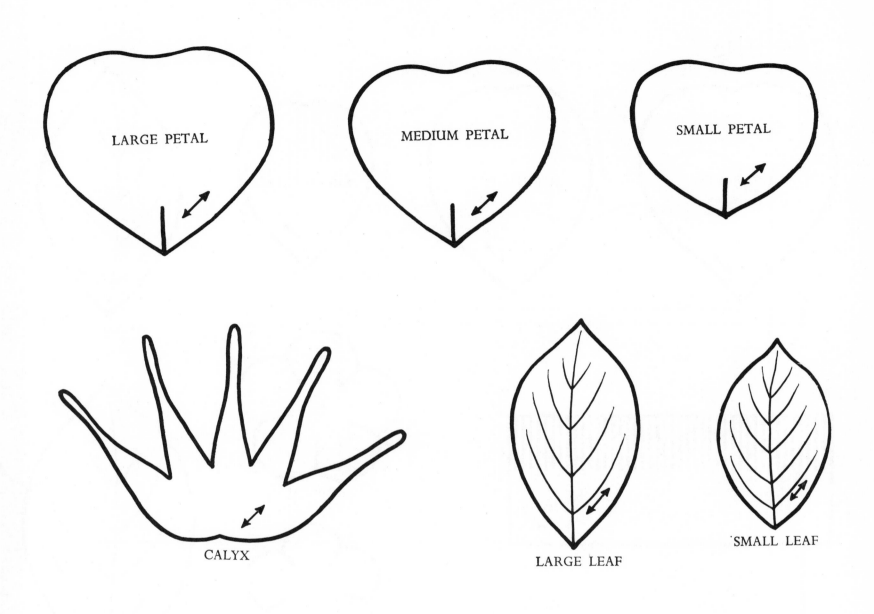

LARGE PETAL

MEDIUM PETAL

SMALL PETAL

CALYX

LARGE LEAF

SMALL LEAF

STEM FABRIC

CAMELLIA

LARGE PETAL

MEDIUM PETAL

SMALL PETAL

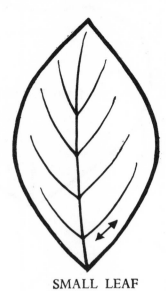

SMALL LEAF

STAMENS

LARGE CALYX

SMALL CALYX

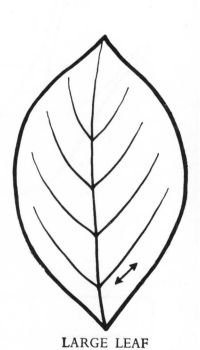

LARGE LEAF

STEM FABRIC (9 in.)

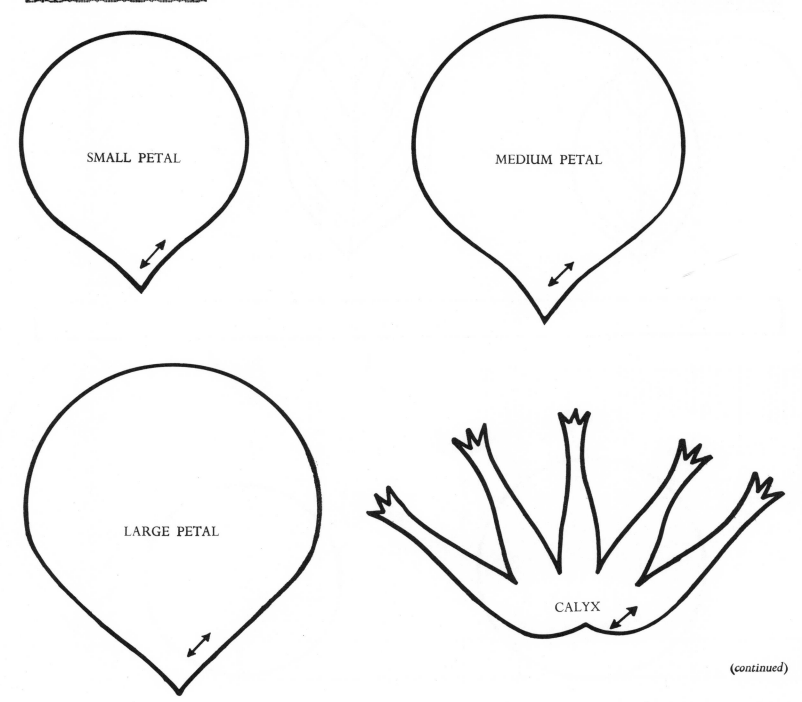

WHITE SWAN ROSE

SMALL PETAL

MEDIUM PETAL

LARGE PETAL

CALYX

(continued)

111

WHITE SWAN ROSE *(continued)*

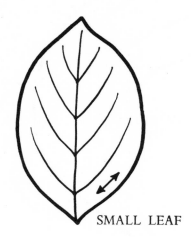

SMALL LEAF

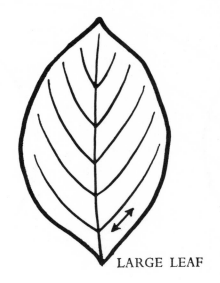

LARGE LEAF

STEM FABRIC

BLACK ROSE

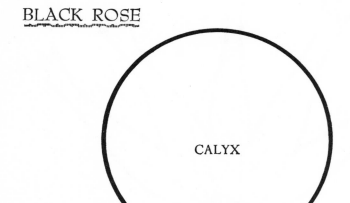

CALYX

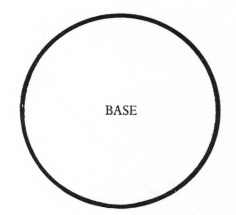

BASE

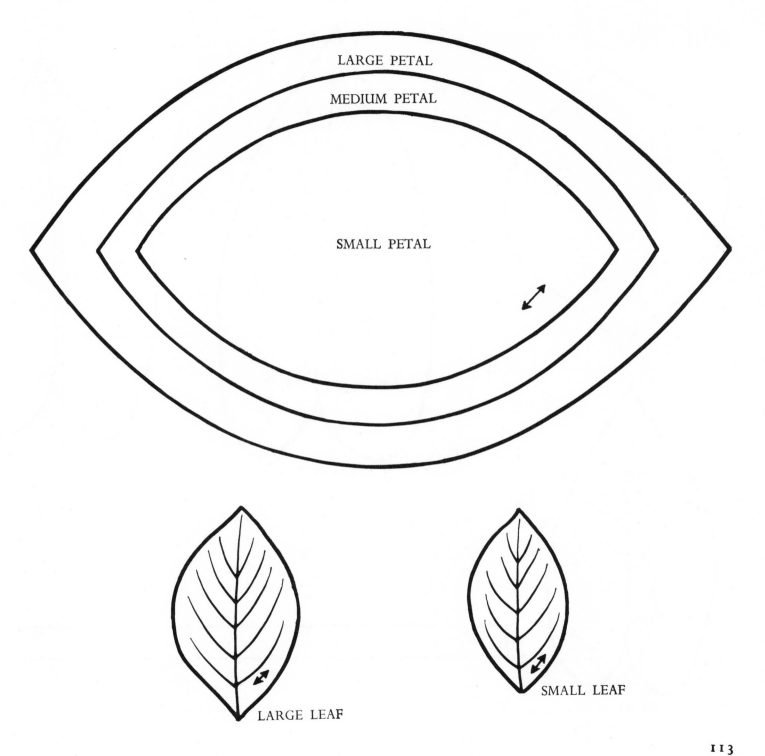

LARGE PETAL

MEDIUM PETAL

SMALL PETAL

LARGE LEAF

SMALL LEAF

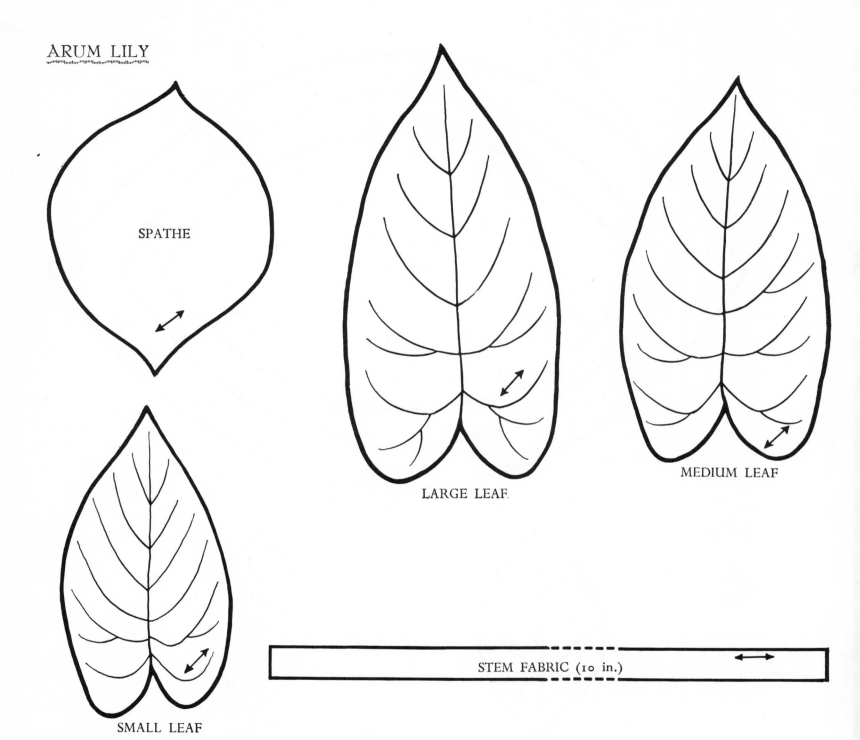

ARUM LILY

SPATHE

LARGE LEAF

MEDIUM LEAF

SMALL LEAF

STEM FABRIC (10 in.)

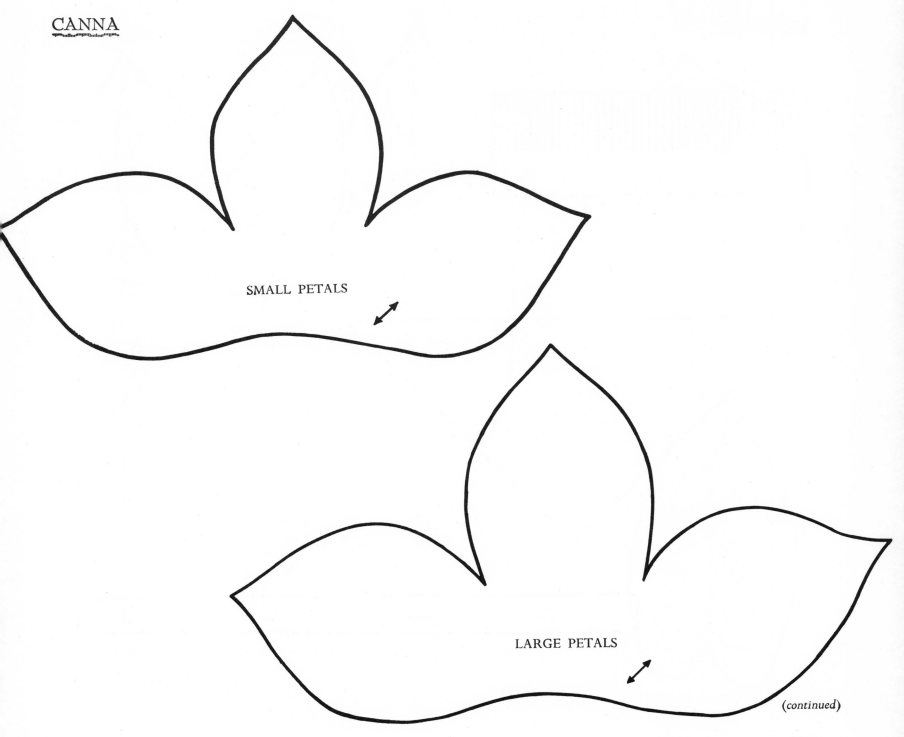

CANNA

SMALL PETALS

LARGE PETALS

(continued)

115

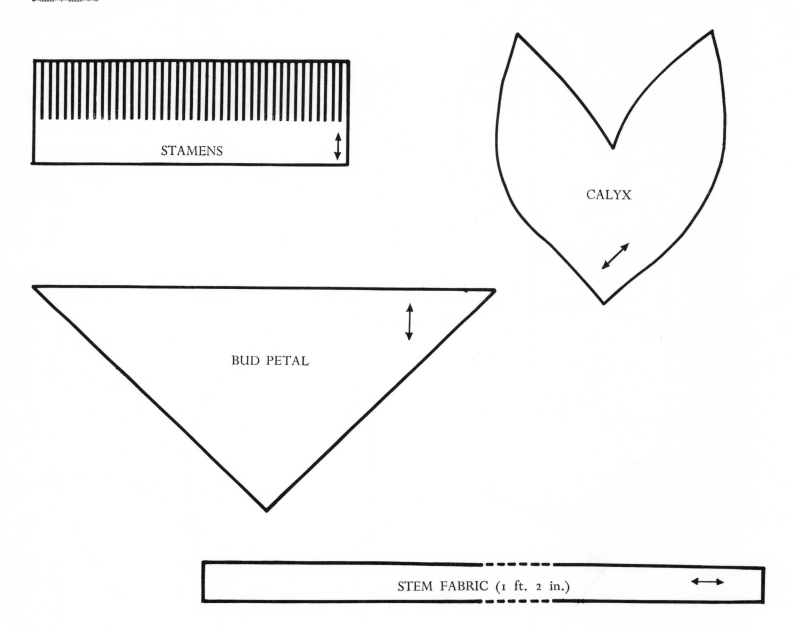

STAMENS

CALYX

BUD PETAL

STEM FABRIC (1 ft. 2 in.)

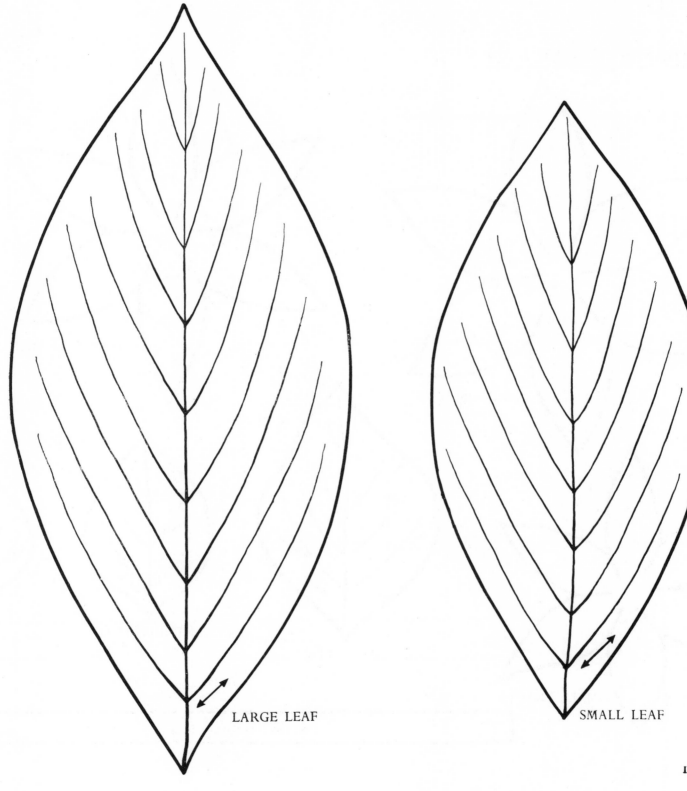

LARGE LEAF

SMALL LEAF

CHINESE LANTERN PLANT

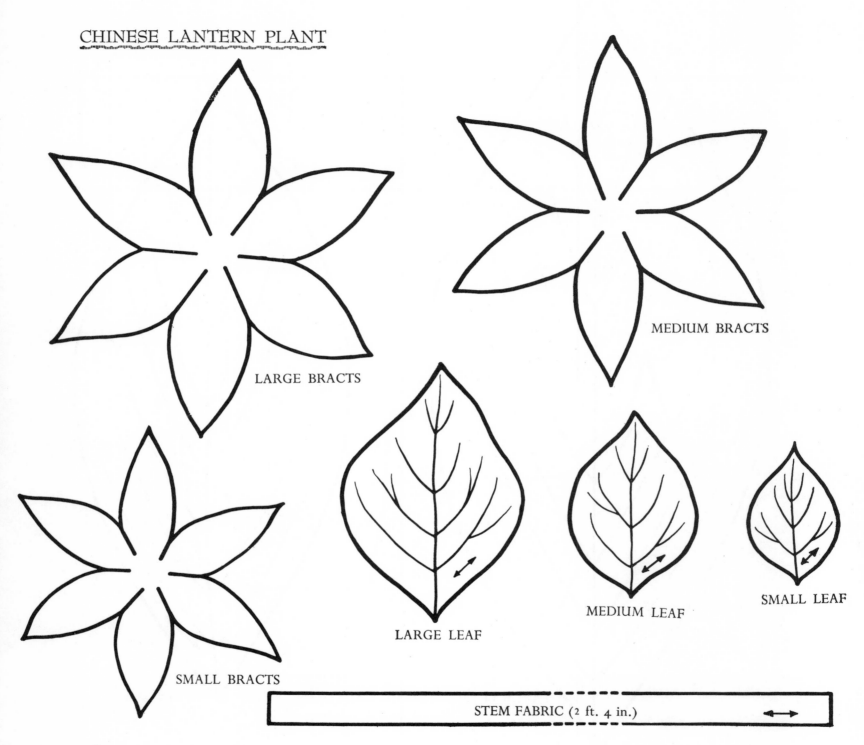

LARGE BRACTS

MEDIUM BRACTS

SMALL BRACTS

LARGE LEAF

MEDIUM LEAF

SMALL LEAF

STEM FABRIC (2 ft. 4 in.)

PINECONE

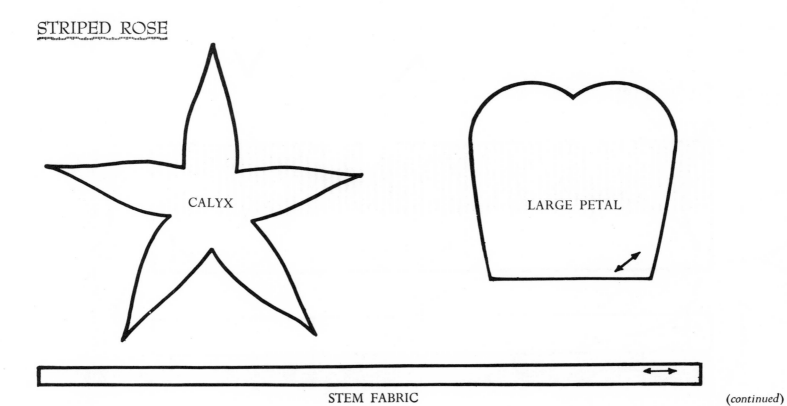

SCALES

STRIPED ROSE

CALYX

LARGE PETAL

STEM FABRIC

(continued)

STRIPED ROSE (*continued*)

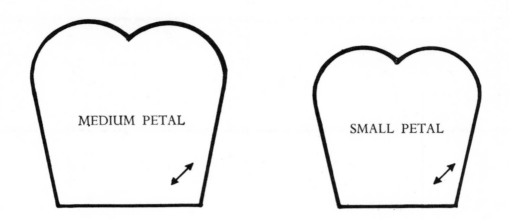

MEDIUM PETAL

SMALL PETAL

ORIENTAL POPPY

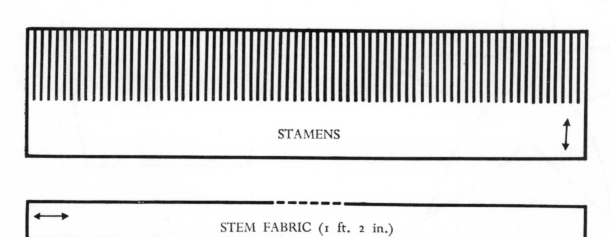

STAMENS

STEM FABRIC (1 ft. 2 in.)

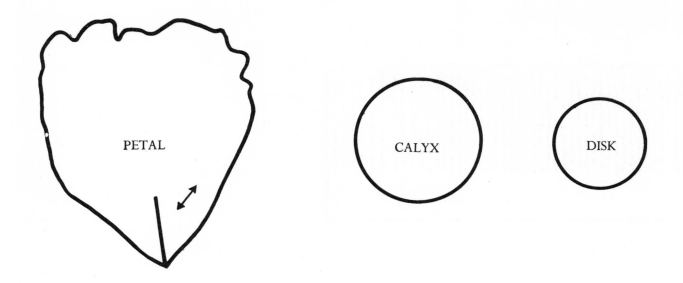

PETAL

CALYX

DISK

GOLD FLOWER

BLACK STAMENS

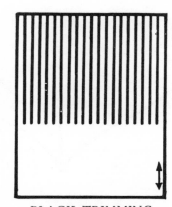

BLACK TRIMMING

(continued)

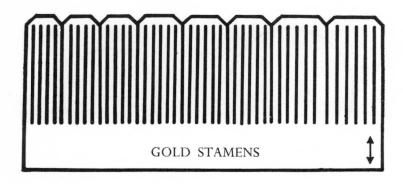

GOLD STAMENS

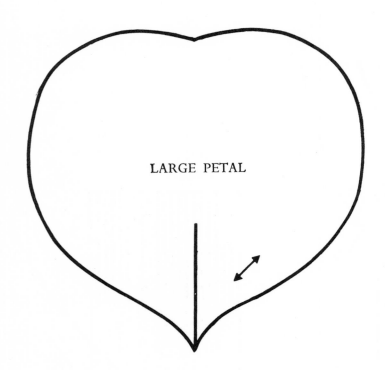

LARGE PETAL

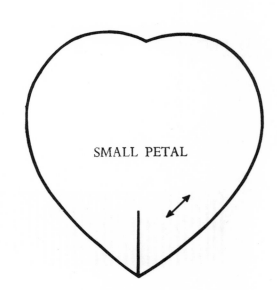

SMALL PETAL

CREPE PAPER ROSE

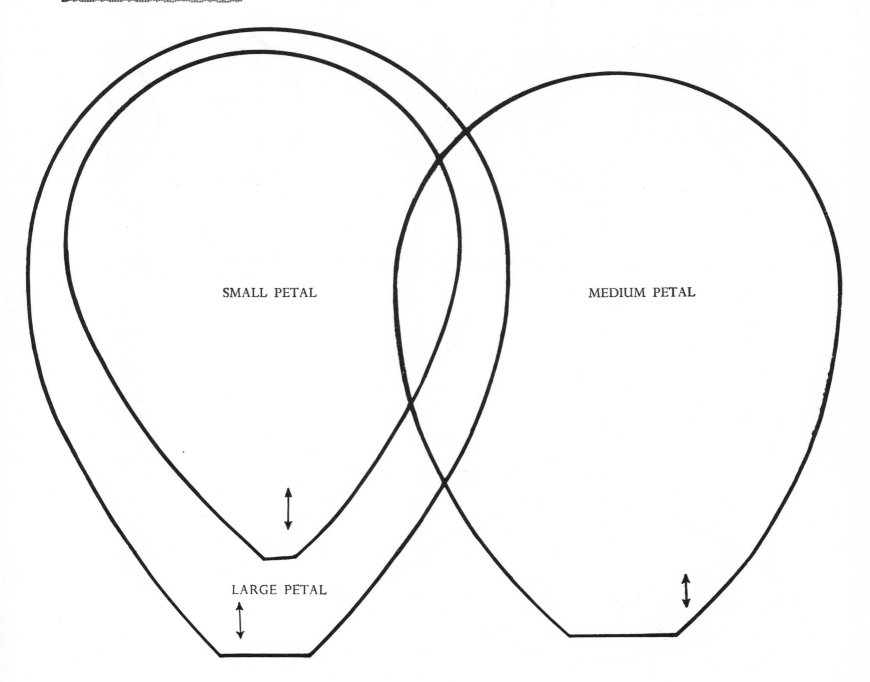

SMALL PETAL

MEDIUM PETAL

LARGE PETAL

SMALL PINK ROSE

SMALL PETAL

LARGE PETAL

CALYX

LARGE LEAF

SMALL LEAF

STEM FABRIC

HEADBAND

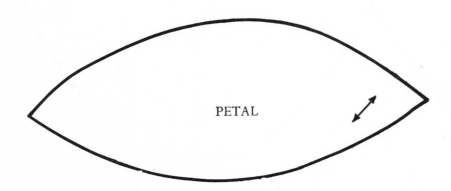

PETAL

124

29 p334
76